The Book of Luck

The Book of Luck

Brilliant ideas for creating your own success and making life go your way

Heather Summers
and Anne Watson

CAPSTONE

First published 2004 by
Capstone Publishing Limited (a Wiley Company)
The Atrium
Southern Gate
Chichester
West Sussex
PO19 8SQ
www.wileyeurope.com
E-mail (for orders and customer service enquires): cs-books@wiley.co.uk

CIP catalogue records for this book are available from the British Library and the US Library of Congress

ISBN 1-84112-635-7

Typeset in Palatino 14/15 pt by Sparks Computer Solutions, Oxford – www.sparks.co.uk
Printed and bound in Great Britain by TJ International Ltd, Padstow, Cornwall
This book is printed on acid-free paper responsibly manufactured from sustainable forestry in which at least two trees are planted for each one used for paper production.

10 9 8 7 6 5 4 3

Contents

---

* This interview analyses Richard's success against all seven Luck Indicators and comments on his answers.

Luck Master Discussions

Acknowledgements

Being lucky people who expect the best from others, we were not the least bit surprised to find that people were overwhelmingly supportive and constructively helpful during the research for *The Book of Luck*. We are grateful to all of the people who have visited (and continue to visit) our website, **www.switchtosuccess.co.uk**, and completed the questionnaire. The data we are collecting there reinforces the theory of our seven Luck Indicators, generating new ideas and possibilities.

Our inspirational role models who feature in the 'Luck Master' discussions and Case Studies were generous with their time and their willingness to share their thoughts and experiences. Their contribution added great value and we thank them for their participation.

Very early on in our research, we discovered that the theme of luck catches everyone's imagination. Everyone seems to have an anecdote, an experience or some knowledge to share with us. All of those e-mails, telephone calls and conversations were invaluable and were appreciated greatly by us – thank you.

John Moseley, our editor at Capstone, tested our Stick-Ability by his frightening confidence in our ability to deliver a manuscript on time. We would like to thank him for the week-ends we spent locked in a cottage in Nidderdale, working out how to hit a deadline while still putting across our passionate belief in people's ability to create a successful life, making the impossible possible.

The real hero of the hour is the one who was our greatest supporter throughout: Herbert the Briard, who attended all of the writing sessions, except for the red wine-fuelled evenings in Italian restaurants when we were pushing ourselves to the outer limits. He remained interested throughout, convinced we were talking great sense and that every word was a pearl of prose. He liked the tea breaks best and is hoping for a sequel, tentatively entitled *Dogged by Good Luck*.

Heather Summers
Anne Watson

Introduction

Chance Your Luck

What is luck?

There is no such thing as luck. This book is not about luck. It is about making the impossible possible and developing a good luck mindset. This book has been inspired by our belief that if people act upon what we set out here, then the word 'average' would disappear. We believe that the world is full of unexplored potential. If you tap into that potential at the individual level, the fluttering of wings will grow into global success.

We consider ourselves to be lucky people – both in our business and our personal lives. We don't do the same things in life or in our work, but we share an upbeat, optimistic view of life that we have turned into a living reality. We have done things we never thought we could. Why has it worked for us when it doesn't always work for others who, at face value, seem to have more going for them? This is a question we have set out to answer in this book.

In our work we interview, assess, train, coach and meet thousands of people. We have a strong focus on building profitable and sustainable businesses that have at their core the desire to help people achieve their potential. Lucky people

1

are successful and successful people are lucky. When we say 'successful', we don't necessarily mean financial success: this is not a 'get rich quick' book. Money is only part of the answer to most people, just as it is all of the answer, or none of the answer, for a minority. We could all be more satisfied with an injection of that 'luck' in our relationships, jobs, day-to-day living and exchanges with others.

What is success?

Success means many different things to many different people. If your goals are financial, then these can range from wanting to make millions to keeping your head above water. If your goals are not financial, then success is likely to be more to do with having peace and harmony in your lives, achieving a work/life balance, having good family relationships, achieving a particular sporting goal, overcoming personal fears or obstacles – or just the satisfaction of living the way that matters to you.

Luck and success

How do 'lucky' people do it? What do they do to achieve success that others don't? We have really enjoyed ourselves during the research for this book, as it gave us the wonderful excuse to meet up with some inspirational people. We explored with them how they have achieved the sort of enviable success that we would all like to have for ourselves. We believe that they are role models who at first glance would seem to have had that tremendous stroke of luck that has somehow passed others by.

They have been kind enough to allow us to include their stories and you will find them scattered throughout this book in our Luck Master discussions or in the Case Studies at the end of the book. Modelling the behaviour of others will pro-vide a shortcut to luck and success.

Have our high flyers been very lucky or do they have extra-ordinary personal qualities we can only wonder at? We will show you ways to emulate some of the things that they are doing instinctively in order to attract that level of good for-tune into your lives.

Research into luck

Our experience and research shows that luck has a clear structure. Thousands of people have visited our website, **www.switchtosuccess.co.uk**, and filled in the Luck Questionnaire. Anyone can improve their luck if they measure themselves against the scale of the Luck Questionnaire and then act.

This broad research has given us the data we need to know that the structure of luck as defined in this book is authentic, substantiated and sound.

How to use this book

This book is simple to follow. Firstly, fill in the Luck Ques-tionnaire on page 8 or via the website (**www.switchtosuccess.co.uk**). This will allow you to compare yourself against the seven Luck Indicators– the seven secrets of success. You can then explore each indicator, giving you Brilliant Ideas on what this could mean for you and what you can do to alter your luck and move towards what success means for you.

Luck and chance

People tend to say 'the harder I work, the luckier I get'. This may be true but it is only a small part of the story: there is more to luck than just hard graft. We will show you brilliant ways to transform your life by transforming your behaviour into that of a lucky person.

Is there a difference between luck and chance? Is there a meaning in coincidence? Chance events are always beyond our control. There is nothing we can do to influence natural disasters such as earthquakes, hurricanes, floods, certain kinds of illness and accidents. Nevertheless, it doesn't stop us from trying – that's why we have a plethora of lucky mascots, good luck charms and rituals, combined with beliefs to help us stave off bad fortune and attract good luck. Even if we don't really think we can affect something as life-critical as a natural disaster or as trivial as the result of a sporting event, we still use our lucky rituals and symbols 'just in case'.

Go on – own up. What do you do and what lucky charms or rituals do you have to rely on to harness the uncertainties of life? By all means hold on to them and to what they mean for you, as long as your dependence on these does not become the reason why you don't take action to improve your lot.

Buying a lottery ticket every week creates in our mind an opportunity to become a millionaire. Depending on that alone to change your financial lot is doomed to failure. The lottery can be a bit of a thrill when the result is announced – a few dreams of what might be and a momentary escape from reality – but that is about all it is.

Create your own luck

The Book of Luck is not about chance – it is about how to create your own luck. If you want to be lucky, remember that it lies in your hands. Even if we can't control events that happen to us, we can control our reaction to them and therefore the results.

As we have already said, choosing to view events as good luck makes the impossible become possible. And the opposite is also true – viewing events as bad luck makes the possible impossible.

And that's what this book is about. Good luck can range from something that has a major impact to minor or insignificant things. We will show you how to break the habits that you have built up in the course of a lifetime and that minor shifts in positions and perspectives can bring surprising rewards. The scope and the depth of the contribution is down to you.

How the questionnaire will help you create your own luck

Our research through the Luck Questionnaire shows that people who have high scores (five or six) on all of the Luck Indicators seem to be consistently successful. It is clear that you can have high scores on six of the indicators, but the seventh could be the mysterious ingredient you have been looking for.

By filling in our questionnaire, you will be able to identify possible gaps in your skill set. The trick to changing your luck is to gain a heightened level of self awareness and then to experiment with our Brilliant Ideas to find out what works for you and what brings meaningful change. By reading this book, you have given yourself the opportunity to look at the world differently. You can decide to commit to doing something you haven't done before and therefore achieve something that you may have thought was beyond your reach.

How this book will help you create your own success and make life go your way

How would you like to feel that your future lies in your hands and you can affect what happens to you? How would you like to know that the place you end up is the place you want to be? There are many different routes and many different options. Perhaps you have narrowed your options and now is the time to see life through a wider lens.

If you have ever asked yourself any of the following questions, then this is the book for you:

❖ Why am I not as lucky as others?
❖ Why does it always happen to me?
❖ Why do I never get the lucky breaks?
❖ Whey don't I get invited to the right places?
❖ Why don't I have a sixth sense?
❖ How can I improve my standard of living?
❖ How can I earn more money?
❖ How can I be more successful?
❖ How do I become more connected?

The Book of Luck will give you ways to answer these questions and discover creative ways to bring more luck into your life.

Brilliant Ideas and the outer limits

At the end of each chapter in this book you will find a section on 'Brilliant Ideas' and 'Brilliant Ideas pushed to the outer limits'. Let's remember that this book is a life-changer if you want it to be. You don't achieve change by fiddling around at the edges. We're not asking you to rearrange the deck chairs on the *Titanic*; we are showing you that by significant alterations in the way you think and the way you behave will bring you better results.

Some of the Brilliant Ideas may seem to you to be a bridge too far. What is normal for some people is wacky to others. When we invite you to use our 'Brilliant Ideas pushed to the outer limits', you are going to have to ask yourself how far you are prepared to go to change your luck. You might want to have a more open mind. You may wish to consider giving yourself permission to experiment and stretch your horizons. Why not be prepared to drop your cynicism and any need for rational thought and proof? Just for a few moments!

The Brilliant Ideas include a menu of tools, techniques and tips that you can use anytime, anyplace and anywhere (or almost!). We are inviting you to try them and decide for yourself which ones are the most likely to increase your luck.

Some of these ideas will work better for you than others. But by trying them all out, you may find that what you may originally have labelled bizarre or irrational somehow becomes part of your routine and part of your luck.

Wherever you are in your life, whether you are just making ends meet or are a millionaire, opening your mind to our Brilliant Ideas will increase your luck.

Choose the things that work for you. Brilliant Ideas make for brilliant lives and brilliant luck.

The Luck Questionnaire

Below you will find 42 statements. Read each one and if you feel it is true for you, mark *A* for 'agree'. If it is not true for you, mark *D* for 'disagree'.

Some choices may be hard, so if you are undecided, be sure to pick the first answer that popped up in your mind. Work quickly and methodically. Be honest.

	Statement	True for you? (A or D)
1	I sometimes feel powerless in the face of things that happen to me	
2	I attribute my good fortune to perseverance and determination	
3	I have always been the sort of person who takes risks and I know I can pull it off	
4	I don't have the control over my emotions that I would ideally like	
5	I find it easy to speak to people I don't know very well	
6	I would describe myself as eternally optimistic – I always see the bright side	
7	No-one knows me better than I know myself	
8	When I'm sorting out a problem, I know that if one way doesn't work, I can always find another	
9	I do not always follow things through to the finish	
10	I love trying out new ideas and experimenting	
11	I spot new ideas in the strangest of places	
12	I find it quite hard getting to know new people	
13	You've got to watch your step, because the world can be an unfriendly place	

Statement	True for you? (A or D)
14 I don't often repeat the same mistake	
15 Where I am in my life is a direct result of all my actions to date	
16 I carry on long after everyone else has given up	
17 I prefer to stay with what I know	
18 I pay attention to what my 'inner voice' is telling me – it seldom lets me down	
19 I chat to strangers when I am out and about	
20 Given the opportunity, most people will take advantage of you	
21 I feel I am a naturally lucky person	
22 I don't allow myself to be at the mercy of chance events	
23 When things go wrong, I can always find another way through	
24 The unknown is an exciting place to be	
25 Whenever coincidences occur in my life, I always look for a deeper meaning	
26 I get on really well with nearly everyone I meet	
27 I can always find a benefit in whatever happens to me, good or bad	
28 I know what I'm good at and where my weaknesses lie	
29 The same situation usually merits a consistent response	

Statement	True for you? (A or D)
30 It preys on my mind if I leave a job unfinished	
31 I am open-minded – I listen to anything	
32 Gut feel plays a very limited part in any decisions I make	
33 I keep in touch with a wide circle of people	
34 Most people are fundamentally good and I trust them	
35 I always welcome feedback from others	
36 When things go against me, I believe that fate plays a significant part	
37 When the going is tough, I know I can find a solution	
38 I like to be with people who challenge my ideas	
39 My decision-making does not always go down the conventional path	
40 I go out of my way to attend social and networking events	
41 I tend to re-run previous difficult events in my mind	
42 I am constantly on the look-out for ways to improve my weak points	

Scoring

Transfer every answer into the relevant box in the answer grid and add up your totals. Score one point for every question box where there are matching letters – i.e. 2 × A or 2 × D.

Answer grid

						Total	Success Skill
1 D	8A	15A	22A	29 D	36 D		Control-Ability
2A	9 D	16A	23A	30A	37A		Stick-Ability
3A	10A	17 D	24A	31A	38A		Risk-Ability
4 D	11A	18A	25A	32 D	39A		Sense-Ability
5A	12 D	19A	26A	33A	40A		Socia-Ability
6A	13 D	20 D	27A	34A	41 D		Percept-Ability
7A	14A	21A	28A	35A	42A		Person-Ability

Interpreting

The answers are grouped together in rows on the answer grid according to which of the seven Luck Indicators they refer to. If your score on any of the rows is four or more, you are already likely to be thinking and behaving in ways that attract luck in these areas. If your score is three or less, there are things you can do to help you to think and behave differently, thus increasing your luck. If you choose to take them on board, your luck will change. More success will come your way.

Good luck!

The seven Luck Indicators

Control-Ability

Control is about choosing and flexing our responses to events and any situation that arises, no matter how difficult it may be. It is an acknowledgement that while we may have no control over events that happen to us, we are fully responsible for our results.

Result? Less blaming the unkind hand of fate. Increased lucky breaks.

Stick-Ability

Stick-Ability is about perseverance, tenacity and following things through – even when the odds are against you. It is about finishing off what you start.

Result? Achieving goals no-one else thought possible.

Risk-Ability

Risk-Ability is the confidence to take a chance rather than plumping for the safe bet, as well as having an open mindset and a willingness to explore and experiment with new ways of thinking and doing things.
Result? More lucky opportunities.

Sense-Ability

Sense-Ability is the skill of using all our senses and feelings to heighten our awareness of lucky opportunities. It includes using our emotional intelligence, gut feel and intuition. It recognises the value of coincidence.
Result? Confidence to rely on inner voice.

Socia-Ability

Socia-Ability is the talent to relate easily to other people in a wide variety of contexts. It includes being comfortable with striking up conversations with people we don't know, being proactive about keeping up with the people we do know and generally going out of our way to network.
Result? More lucky coincidences.

Percept-Ability

Percept-Ability is all about how we look at life, events, ourselves and others. Do we have good expectations? Do we always see (or at least search for) the positive side of negative events or people? Is our attitude to life optimistic? Do we shrug off small worries and concerns? If we do, this is true Percept-Ability!

Result? Bad luck is turned into good luck.

Person-Ability

Person-Ability is about knowing ourselves well enough to recognise what works well for us and what can work against us. This self-awareness is the skill to use those aspects of our personality that will naturally support us in being lucky.

Result? The harnessing of all our natural luck skills.

Luck Master 1: Colin Tucker

I knew Colin Tucker was going to have strong views on luck before we even talked about it. Surely I was about to find that the Deputy Chairman of Hutchison 3G, a Chinese-owned business with a telephone number made up of the Chinese numbers that signify luck and fortune, relied on external forces?

Colin believes that luck is made up of chance and opportunities, and is constructed by the extent to which you take up the opportunities that arise. I asked him if he thought of himself as a lucky person. He believes that he is and is very firm in his belief that this started at an early age. When he was five years old he had an engineer's mind, starting out with a Meccano set and always gaining pleasure from knowing how things worked. He doesn't know where this mindset came from as he does not come from a family of engineers – it just happened. He chanced to be an engineer. He always had something that he enjoyed doing and then he had the opportunities to encompass it in his working life. I wanted

14

to know what his definition of luck and success was and he is clear that it is more than financial reward: there has to be satisfaction included. Colin enjoys life and the satisfaction he gets is an integral part of his everyday working life.

I was beginning to panic at this point, as I could not see how satisfaction fitted our model of luck. I decided to ask about bad luck, to see if Colin's views there might help me out there. He said that unlucky things in life were often actually the opposite: you have to take the knocks and convert them into something that is positive. 'Be flexible and stay positive,' he says, 'otherwise you won't go anywhere.' What a relief – Colin may not know it but he has strong Percept-Ability.

I found it hard to look on Colin as an engineer, since he does not fit the stereotype of the typical engineer, the person who is more interested in machines, technology and mechanics than people. He loves engineering and embraces new technologies but overriding all of this is his love of interacting with people. He reckons that he knows first-class engineers who have not made an impact in career terms because ironically, the qualities that make them good engineers hold them back. Add the ability to go out and meet people to a good engineer and you have a recipe for success. If you want to get on in life, according to Colin, you have to be reasonably networked so that your name pops up in places and opportunities come your way. That's the way the headhunter knows who you are and gives you a call. That's how Colin got one of his top jobs. I could scarcely conceal my glee – it was Socia-Ability.

Colin doesn't consider himself to be a risk-taker, so I decided to explore this with him a little more. Although Colin would never jump at the first opportunity that came along, he is ready to move once he has analysed things. When he decided to leave GPT in 1991 to join Orange, a colleague told him that he was out of his mind and would be out of work within three months. Instead it proved to be a stunning career opportunity that transformed his life. He had the satisfaction of being part of the success of Orange combined with financial reward.

Colin still thinks that enjoying what you do is the key to good luck and success. Whenever he has found himself in a situation where he was not enjoying himself, he changed what he was doing. He believes that there is no longer a job for life, so it is important treat everyone in the same way and be polite to people across all levels. Business is about being human, so it must be underpinned by integrity and honesty. Colin's style is to ensure that he tells people the core of the truth, not just what they need to know to get through. Colin knows himself well and knows what the components of job satisfaction are. He has clarity of style, objectives and values, so high-scoring Person-Ability is a key component.

Colin may consider himself to be a lucky person, but a careful look shows us that he knows how to take his chances. He has a natural zest for life and keen interest in new and untested things.

When we said our farewells, Colin was off to Warwickshire to do an exam in instruments the next day, part of his pilot's licence for his private plane. 'You still say you are not a risk-taker, then?' I asked.

He looked puzzled. 'Of course not.'

Control – Ability

'We can let circumstances rule us or we can take charge
and rule our lives from within' – Earl Nightingale

Control is about choosing and flexing our responses to events and any situation that arises, no matter how difficult it may be. It is an acknowledgement that while we may have no control over events that happen to us, we are fully responsible for our results.

Result? Less blaming the unkind hand of fate. Increased lucky breaks.

Control – Ability and what it means for you

This secret is fundamental; it underpins all the others. It's about how you can make the most of every situation that happens and therefore attract more luck into your life.

If you want to know more about Control-Ability, read Case Studies 1 (page 192), 4 (page 208) and 7 (page 222)

If you master the art of being in charge of your own life and make the most of every situation that occurs, then you will attract more luck into your life. Whingeing will vanish. Not for you the feeling of being 'stabbed in the back' or 'punched in the stomach' – you are in charge, you are free and the world is at your feet. You can do anything you choose to do and the world is your oyster.

If you take control then, you will create your own luck rather than being the victim of bad luck. Control means assuming 100% responsibility for everything that happens to you in your life. You will be the lucky person who says, 'I know I am in control of my own life. I am pretty good at getting where I want to be.'

Control-Ability means being *At Choice* in life. This doesn't mean that we are able to choose or control everything that happens to us; what it does mean is that we always have a choice about how to respond to any event or situation that occurs in our lives. Being able to choose our response has a huge impact on our results and therefore our luck.

The 'Sleeping Beauty' mindset

The opposite of Control-Ability is the 'Sleeping Beauty' type of mentality that is the theme of many traditional children's stories. Sleeping Beauty is entirely dependent on her handsome prince to awaken her to life and happiness. Poor old Sleeping Beauty: first of all she has to lie comatose waiting to be awoken by a prince and then she meekly marries a complete stranger.

You don't want to be one of these people waiting forever to be rescued, do you? You don't wait for the lottery results every Saturday, thinking you might have won and that your life will transform, do you? You don't think you will hit it rich by finding a rich partner who will whisk you off on a magic carpet to a life of carefree luxury, do you?

Billy Bunter spent a long time waiting for his postal order and in the process became a laughing stock. Mr McCawber waited for something to turn up and became a watchword for hopeless inaction.

In many of the books giving advice to parents on how to bring up their children, it is suggested that children are en-couraged to s-t-r-e-t-c-h for what they want. At a very early age, objects are put just within reach and not simply handed to the child. The same principle applies later on in life. If we want our luck to improve, we need to take action; we need to take control of life and not wait for life to make the moves.

Suppose your son or daughter runs up an overdraft and can't find a way to pay it without significant extra work or effort. Is the best thing to bail them out and pay off the debt – or to leave them to find their own solution? The easiest route if you have the money is to pay it off, tell them off and hope they have learnt the lesson. According to the Citizen's Advice Bureau, however, the best route is to allow the person who has run up the debt to find the money to pay it back. You spent it – you sort it.

The 'wooden leg' mindset

There are people who don't grab life by the short and curl-ies and are not seeking and finding new ways to forge their own destiny or success. Other people expect money, success, happiness as their right. If it doesn't happen, they can become resentful. They are likely to play the destructive psychologi-cal game of 'wooden leg' described by Eric Berne in the book *What Do You Say After You Say Hello?* In it, an excuse is used

19

to 'explain' why someone has not been able to do something. The language goes something like this:

❖ If it wasn't for this wooden leg, I would be/have been able to climb that mountain.
❖ If it wasn't for my health, I would have reached a more senior position in my career.
❖ If I hadn't been the youngest person in my school year I would have won more prizes.
❖ If it wasn't for my divorce I would have been better off.
❖ If I had more money I would be happy.
❖ Unless my bonus is more than last year's, I'll be very disappointed.

The 'success' mindset

In each case, how the person feels is dependent on outside circumstances. They are at the mercy of events or occurrences that may well be outside their control.

A recent study of entrepreneurs demonstrates that those with strong levels of Control-Ability were generally more successful in running their businesses. They never attribute their success to luck but claim it as their own.

They know that their key skills, such as perseverance, good decision making, willingness to go that extra mile, readiness to take risks, hard work and their own talents, are the vital ingredients for their apparent 'luck'.

In the same study, interviews with entrepreneurs who had a failed business behind them tended to blame external factors such as economic downturn, poor suppliers, unsupportive banks, poorly performing employees and bad luck. They tended to say things like 'If it had not been for …'. Their assumption was that control was out of their reach. Unlucky and unsuccessful people push control outside themselves and ascribe their lack of success to outside influences and events.

Reasons or excuses

Success is rarely handed to you on a plate. The first step towards managing your life and managing your luck, and being in real control, is being aware of situations and contexts when you slip into comfortable behavioural patterns and where it is easier to sidestep full responsibility.

Have you ever considered any of the following statements – or similar – to be acceptable?

- ❖ The business went down because of cash flow.
- ❖ If that car hadn't braked so suddenly, I wouldn't have crashed into the back of it.
- ❖ If he had not been so selfish, our relationship would not have failed.
- ❖ I would be slimmer and fitter if only I had the time to go to the gym.
- ❖ I had to resign because they did not make me feel part of the team.
- ❖ He made me feel angry.
- ❖ Bad weather always makes me feel miserable.
- ❖ Her remarks make me feel inadequate.
- ❖ We had a dreadful evening because the food in the restaurant was so bad.
- ❖ I could do so much more if only I enjoyed better health.
- ❖ If only I had gone to university or a good school – I would have had a much better job.
- ❖ I'll feel fulfilled when I have a family.

❖ If no-one thanks me for what I've done, I feel unappreciated.

At first glance, these might appear to be very good reasons to explain something that has gone wrong. In truth, they are *excuses*: they are conditional on external factors.

Are you the fish or the fisherman?

You may sometimes hear this opposite side of being in control described as being *At Effect*. Think of the fisherman who has a fish at the end of his line. The fish is under the fisherman's control, being played at the end of the line. It is powerless: it is At Effect and being jerked along by factors outside itself. We have the choice to be the fish or the fisherman in all the different areas of our lives.

Lucky people are those who are in control and embrace responsibility in more aspects of their lives than unlucky people.

Being At Choice and accepting 100% responsibility for all of our actions does not mean blaming ourselves when things go wrong. The trick about Control-Ability is to balance and embrace two seemingly opposite notions

These are:

❖ be 100% responsible for whatever you say and do; and
❖ be kind to yourself because wherever you go, there you are.*

Being 100% responsible, or At Cause, is like driving your own bus and not letting anyone else do that for you. It means

---

* From the film *The Adventures of Buckaroo Banzai Across the 8th Dimension*

accepting that where you are in your life is a direct result of all the decisions you have (or have not) taken. It means not pointing the finger outwards and blaming fate, others or external events for where you are in life.

Being kind to yourself means *not* beating yourself up for mistakes you have made or feeling guilty about things you have done. It does not mean being complacent; it means learning from your mistakes in such a way that you can be freed up. It means not pointing the finger inward and blaming yourself.

True Control-Ability, therefore, means being At Cause or At Choice. The more we are At Choice in what we do, the more personal power we will have in our lives and the better able we are to be successful in whatever way we choose.

What about events outside our control?

There are some events over which we may have little or no control. There are occasions when we slip into the realm of chance, when events happen that are truly beyond our control. These include:

- ❖ death;
- ❖ disaster;
- ❖ illness;
- ❖ chance happenings;
- ❖ terrorist attacks;
- ❖ accidents;
- ❖ theft and burglary;
- ❖ fraud;
- ❖ weather;
- ❖ inherited traits;
- ❖ redundancy;

- ❖ debt;
- ❖ divorce;
- ❖ bankruptcy; and
- ❖ other people's behaviour.

An important step towards managing our life and our luck, and being in real control, is choosing how we *respond* to situations that are genuinely outside our control.

We may not have control over the events themselves, but we do have control over how to *respond* to them. We can therefore choose to react to life's events so that we can achieve a better and a luckier result.

Think of it like the following formula:

$$S + R = C$$

Or: Situation plus Response leads to Consequence.

One way to look at it is shown in Figure 1.1.

The level of our ability to respond appropriately, actively and creatively to events will determine our results. This ability to respond is a key factor in Control-Ability – as, of course, is choice.

We can only control our outcome, our results, our luck, by the quality of the response we *choose*.

John and Chris worked together in the same team. They were made redundant at the same time. John decided to treat the event as an opportunity to reassess what he wanted from his life and his career. He set up an 'office' at home and treated job-hunting as if it were his full-time occupation. He decided what was important to him in his life and in his work and set

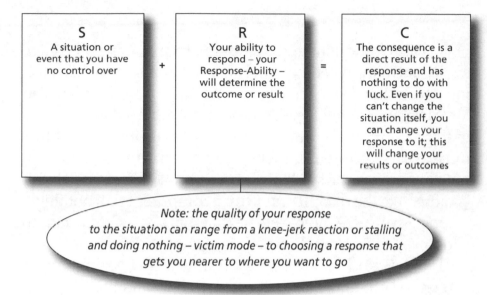

Figure 1.1   *Situation plus Response leads to Consequence*

out to find a job that would match his criteria. Five months later, after many setbacks, he was working in a job that gave him the life balance he wanted. He is happier, more fulfilled and no worse off than before

Chris was devastated by being made redundant – he felt victimised. He had always given his all to the company and felt that being made redundant was not fair. He browsed the job pages for the first month but rapidly became dejected after several rejections for interview. The number of job applications he sent decreased by the month. Eight months on he still has no job – and no prospect of one. He is sad, resentful and in debt.

Two very different responses to the same event. Two very different consequences.

To choose or not to choose - that is the question!

It is also important to recognise that *not* making a positive choice and simply letting things happen is a fast track to ending up a victim. Have there been times, for example, when you have let things slide? When you have not gone out of your way to follow up an opportunity because you have been too busy, too tired, too stressed? Or when you haven't made a decision but you bemoan the fact that the opportunity has slipped by? It is rather like the default option on a computer to do nothing.

Being truly At Choice means that it is just as important to choose *not* to do something as it is to choose do it.

'I understand that taking control means choosing my response to situations that occur in my work and life,' you say. 'However, sometimes I can't help myself. It's not easy to *choose* what to say or do in difficult situations. After all, I'm only human!'

The fact is that we can all 'help ourselves' if we want to enough, and if and when we choose to.

Why do we not always respond in the way we want?

How does it come about that we don't respond to tricky situations as well as we'd like to? There are many possible reasons why we respond badly. Perhaps it's because:

- ❖ that's the way our parents always did it;
- ❖ that's the way that we've got into the habit of responding because it has worked for us in the past;
- ❖ that's our assumption of 'how it is', 'how things are' and what is 'true';
- ❖ we don't know a better way, so we don't know what to do differently – or we don't have the skill;

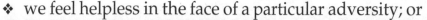

- ❖ we feel helpless in the face of a particular adversity; or
- ❖ we are just having a run of bad luck.

This book is for those who really want to find a better way and make positive changes in their lives. To do that you need to recognise that flexibility of behaviour is a key part of a person who makes the choice.

Consider what would happen if you could use your Control-Ability to create your own success.

Create your own success: create Control-Ability

What will happen if you don't have Control-Ability?

If you are not in control of your life and your response to what happens to you then you are likely to act the victim, blaming others for your dissatisfactions. It will feel like you are a puppet, with someone else pulling your strings in that part of your life. As a consequence, you may well feel that you are unable to change.

You will feel powerless with stress and unhappiness in the face of life's events.

You may well become one of life's moaners, complaining about your lot and feeling unable to do anything about it.

What won't happen if you don't have Control-Ability?

When you don't have Control-Ability, you lose the capacity to bring about change in your life. You won't believe that change is possible. You will find it hard to resist the will of others and, as a consequence, you will lack any structure in your life because you have no control over it.

- ❖ You won't be able to change your job.
- ❖ You won't be able to change your financial status.
- ❖ You won't be able to improve the relationships in your life.
- ❖ You won't be able to get on with life the way you'd like to lead it.

What won't happen if you do have Control-Ability?

You won't believe that other people can affect the course and direction of your life.

Unhappiness often stems from the feeling of being a victim. This will never be felt by people who have high Control-Ability, because they see themselves as responsible for all the results in their life – good and bad.

What will happen if you do have Control-Ability?

When you take responsibility for your life and your luck you know that you will reap what you sow. Whatever happens to you, you will see it as a consequence of your own actions and your own thoughts.

You will enjoy the positive feeling that comes from choosing your own way in life and your own destiny.

If you choose to be At Cause or At Choice, all things will seem possible and within your grasp.

Make life go your way

The effects of having or not having Control-Ability are shown in Table 1.1.

Table 1.1   *Make life go your way*

What will happen if you do have Control-Ability?	What will happen if you don't have Control-Ability?
You will be in control of your destiny	You will feel stressed
You will feel positive	You will feel powerless
You will know that you reap what you sow	You will feel that other people are pulling your strings
You will enjoy the knowledge that you are the person who chooses your own route and your own destiny	You will act the victim

What won't happen if you don't have Control-Ability?	What won't happen if you do have Control-Ability?
You won't have control over your own life	You won't leave things to chance
You won't have any structure to your life	You won't sit back and wait for things to happen
You won't believe that you have the ability to influence your life	You won't waste time
You won't be able to change anything	You won't be able to blame other people
You won't be able to resist the will of others	You will never see yourself as a victim
You won't be able to effect any changes	

Brilliant Ideas for using Control-Ability to increase your luck

Here is a way to reinforce the notion that the ability to be flexible is a key part of creating your own luck. Strong levels of Control-Ability will enable you to make positive changes in your life. Flexibility of style gives you the ability to choose the sort of response that is most likely to get you the outcome you want.

This does *not* mean giving in and being a doormat, or allowing yourself to be run roughshod over. This would not produce a win/win situation – it would result in a situation where someone else wins and you lose.

Neither is it about trampling through the undergrowth and hacking at everything and everyone in your path until you get what you want. This would result in a win/lose outcome – a win for you and a loss for others.

If you are already lucky and successful but feel that you have the potential to do more, have more or be more of who you really are, then read on. If you feel that life has, in the past, dealt you a poor hand and that now is the time to change your future, then here is your opportunity to find new and better ways to change your luck and change your fortune.

Flexibility of response means being courageous and creative enough to change your behaviour in a way that is most likely to achieve a result that is good for you and for others.

Here are some Brilliant Ideas on how to take control of your response to events.

How to think before speaking

Think of situations in the past where you have said something that you regretted afterwards. Replay these situations in your mind and in each one, just before you said the thing you later regretted, imagine yourself taking a deep breath and heard yourself saying something like: '*Stop!* What outcome do I want from this – and what is the best thing to say or do now?'

How to stay positive

Stand up straight – as tall as you can while staying in perfect balance. Look up and smile. It's hard to be miserable or sad in this posture.

Remember! The mind and the body are part of the same system. If our body feels good, so does our mind. If we feel good in ourselves, our body reflects that.

How to learn from mistakes

Review other situations when you have not got the result you wanted. You may even have got the opposite! Write down, with the benefit of hindsight, what would have been better. Jot these down in a notebook so that you can refer to them when you need them.

How to control the future: the visual rehearsal

Imagine an up-and-coming situation that you are apprehensive about – one where normally you might rehearse in your head what was likely to happen and what might go wrong. We call this 'catastrophising'.

What exactly do we mean by catastrophising? We've probably all done it. For example, have you ever worried when someone dear to you is home late? You keep checking your watch, looking out of the window, checking your mobile for messages, pacing the floor – and as the minutes tick by, you think of all the terrible things that could have happened. By the time the door opens and the person arrives, you are in a state of panic and have had them mentally dead and buried. You can see that this response to an event that you have no control over is not a useful one: you are projecting a potentially negative outcome and

31

upsetting yourself, with all the accompanying physical symptoms, yet all this is a product of your imagination. This illustrates beautifully the power of the mind and the imagination.

This power can be used equally well with a positive benefit. Visualising is a natural skill we all have, yet we seldom put it to positive use.

Instead of imagining the worst, pretend that you are your own film director. Picture yourself making a movie of yourself in the situation you are not looking forward to. Because you are the director, you can cut and edit and produce exactly the movie that you want.

Do this now. Picture an imaginary screen and see yourself on that screen. Visualise the situation and see yourself, responding and acting in free-flow the way you've always dreamed. Make the colours more attractive – brighter and sharper, for example. Adjust the focus and try to make your picture nearer. See the whole episode running successfully from beginning to end so that you end up with a win/win result. If your picture becomes negative at any stage, simply rewind the film in your head and picture it again until you get the one you want.

Once you have completed your film, rewind it, play it through, and feel great knowing that it will have a brilliant ending. Play this 'tape' in your mind's eye many times before the actual event.

The reason this always works is because the mind is not always able to tell the difference between the past and the future. A compelling visual rehearsal programs a successful outcome into your neurology. Your picture is different, your expectations are different and your confidence greater. The signals you transmit unconsciously will be helpful and you'll find it easier to choose your response.

We are more naturally inclined to catastrophise than to visualise in a positive way. Consider your mind to be a garden. If you neglect a garden, the flowers quickly disappear. It becomes choked with weeds, the lawn becomes knee high and the whole garden just goes to seed. We need to look after our minds and our imagination in the same way as we would a well-tended garden. Visualising is a positive technique that gives control.

More visualisation

Here's another example of how we can use visualisation to change an outcome. Have you ever been in a position when you have had to give a speech at a wedding, a farewell dinner or a conference? Take the example of Wendy, who was asked to make a speech at her daughter's 21st birthday celebrations. Wendy was a successful businesswoman and confident in many different situations, but speech-making was not one of them. She was dreading standing in front of relatives, friends and colleagues. She could have catastrophised and imagined making, at best, a boring speech and, at worst, making a fool of herself. Instead, she decided to visualise the whole process from start to finish. She imagined herself to be relaxed and confident. She saw looks of appreciation and heard the laughter, the applause and the congratulations on a witty, humorous speech that was well delivered. In the event, many people told her afterwards it was the best speech they had ever heard.

Here are some more specific techniques that you are invited to try on. See how you feel about them and discover if they make sense to you.

How to control through language

Language can be used to help us take control of ourselves

as well as others, and therefore achieve better outcomes and increase our luck.

With language, it is important to remember that the same words can mean different things to different people. By taking control of how we use our written and spoken language, we can influence the way others feel and act. Language does not just affect the person with whom we are communicating; the words we use influence the way we feel and the results we can create for ourselves. Thoughtful use of language can increase our luck.

Here are some of the negative word patterns in common usage:

❖ I should do this/I should not do this.
❖ I ought to have done that/I ought not to have done that.
❖ I must go there/I must not go there.
❖ It is necessary for me to …
❖ I will try to achieve this.

Why are these unhelpful?

'Should', 'might', 'must' and 'necessary' are other people's imperatives. This is the language of people who are At Effect. It is not the language of people who are At Choice or In Control. If you find yourself using some of this language, you can challenge yourself in the following ways:

❖ Why not?
❖ Who says?
❖ What will happen if I did?
❖ What will happen if I didn't?
❖ What wouldn't happen if I did?
❖ What wouldn't happen if I didn't?

'Should', 'ought', 'must' and 'have to' can cause stress in life: they bring with them the burden of other people's expectations. Simply using language such as 'I choose to' or 'I choose not to' can have a radically liberating effect because you are in control once more. People who are in control consciously say 'I choose to', 'I choose not to', 'I don't want to', 'I would like to' 'I have decided to' or 'I have decided not to'. Being In Control liberates; being At Effect causes stress.

This is also the case for the word 'try', which suggests huge effort without necessarily achieving the goal. Try to raise your right arm. See? Either you can lift it or you can't. You don't have to put in the huge amount of effort implied by the word 'try'. Are you convinced when someone says 'I will try to get that to you by the following date'? Embedded in the word 'try' is the expectation of failure.

How to prepare for being caught broadside on: the snapshot

The trick with this technique is to practise it before unexpected events hit. People who are in control prepare themselves for the unexpected.

The snapshot technique will not only give you the resources to cope with unexpected difficulties but will also help you remove anxiety and increase your self-esteem. The more control you have over your emotions and the way you react, the more your luck will increase.

Have you ever carried a snapshot of a loved one around with you in your wallet? Perhaps you used to. And perhaps you looked at it from time to time and felt good when you did so.

This exercise enables you to carry a snapshot of yourself around with you, taken at a time when you were at your most calm, peaceful and resourceful. Think of a time when you were completely relaxed and at one with the world. Relive and recapture the feelings you had at that time. Remember how easily and calmly you breathed. Feel the pleasure. Adjust the colour, brightness focus and distance of the picture you have in your mind until it's just how you want it.

When the feeling is at its peak, look at yourself in the mirror and capture it, then click as if you were taking a photograph. Then put the photograph inside your mind in a place where you know you will be able to retrieve it any time you want it. Practise getting the mental photograph to look at four or five times so that you become good at it.

The next time something stressful knocks you unexpectedly, simply access your snapshot. You will feel calm, in control and more able to take charge of the situation.

A good way to practise this exercise would be to ask a trusted friend to do something to shock you such as clapping their hands loudly or shouting at you, so that you can become good at bringing the picture to mind almost automatically

You will notice how good it is to have that much control over your feelings. Experience tells us that the people who are able to do this well are better able to keep a positive mindset. This allows them to take control of situations more readily and in the process, stack the deck of luck.

Brilliant Ideas pushed to the outer limits

How to make the phone ring

This is an example of how it is possible to control communication. Has there ever been an occasion when you waited anxiously for the phone to ring? How would it be if you could cause someone to pick up the phone and get in touch when you wanted them to?

We know this happens naturally between people who are in tune. Take Benjamin and William, for instance. They are close friends who share the details of their lives with each other. In one month alone, they counted seven separate occasions when they communicated simultaneously: they both lifted the phone to each other at the same time, a text message crossed with a voicemail message, and so on.

To access this capability with the people you want, firstly, imagine the person you want to call you. Picture them as clearly as you can, looking at their telephone and thinking about calling you. Imagine your energy reaching out to them and coming back in a loop to you.

Some people find that when they start this process, the energy has the feeling of being fragmented and they know the connection has been made when the energy feels smooth and goes round in the loop easily. Don't be surprised when the person calls you up and tells you that for some reason they felt the need to call! Most people would ascribe this to luck, but you will know that you have made your own luck.

Anne and Martin sat in the main square of Cordoba enjoying the warm sunshine and sipping a cortado coffee. They remembered the previous year when they had been at the same table having dinner with a close friend Gareth. The memory was powerful, as the evening had been a particularly special one, including all of the key ingredients – food, wine, music and good companionship. As they remembered it, Anne glanced at her mobile phone and it began to ring. It was Gareth.

How to control someone else's luck

This exercise supports people who are going through an important event in their lives, such as an interview, an examination, an operation signing a vital document or reacting to an important e-mail.

Take the example of your son sitting a vital exam. Collect together the people who wish him well. Join hands in a circle and think of him opening the question paper. Picture him smiling as he reads the questions. Hear him thinking, 'Wow, this is easy – I can do this'. Send him the collective energy of the group to see him through the exam so that he can give of his best. Of course one person can do this, but it is the combined resources of the group that make it particularly effective.

How to park your car

One of the biggest challenges when driving is finding somewhere to park the car when you decide to stop – it can make you late, bring you stress and find you parking tickets. Have you ever driven round, unable to find a single spot but knowing you just have to go to the bank, get to a meeting or pick up a child on time?

Forget those days – they are gone forever. Before you set off, take time to think of where you are going and where you would like to park. We always like a spot that doesn't require wild manoeuvrings to get into, attracting an audience of superior beings who always park perfectly first time.

Have a picture in your mind of that marvellous spot, where you can just glide in and be handy for that meeting afterwards. Got it? Now see yourself driving into it with a sigh of satisfaction that your personal space was waiting for you. See it clearly and leave it there, empty and waiting for you just as you drive up. You no longer need to rely on luck for finding a parking place – create your own before you leave.

Because visualising works on parking spots, just imagine what else it could do for you!

A friend, Maria, had been very ill and was moving house just as she was reaching the end of a tough course of chemotherapy. Before she moved we suggested that she could take an old tin and take the lid off it. We then invited her to think of the cancer, see it, shrink it to a tiny size and then put in the tin, placing the lid firmly on the top and sealing it permanently. She could then move house knowing she had left her illness behind, forgotten at the back of an old shed or dumped unceremoniously off a cliff.

The shredder

Take control of your worries. Write them down. If you own or have access to a shredder, take delight in shredding them to oblivion. If you don't have a shredder, simply tear them up into tiny pieces or imagine you have a shredder and picture them being reduced to nothing. In this way you face the worst but put it behind you.

Imagine the power of this if you use it for worries and concerns that are, at first glance, beyond your control.

So what's stopping you getting in control? Lucky people are in control of their lives and can choose how lucky they are.

Luck Master 2: Richard Brewster

Tessa the black Labrador was not impressed by our debates on the influence of luck in the life of Richard Brewster. She sighed, yawned and gazed longingly at the plate of cake, finding the attractions of food infinitely more exciting than the considerations of luck. Tessa has hit it lucky, living in the Richard's West London family home: she is surrounded by a loving family, the cupboards are full of food and the master of the house is a self-acclaimed 'lucky man' who knows that life has gone his way.

Meet Richard Brewster: *Guardian* Young Businessman of the Year 1990, former chief executive of two PLCs and currently enjoying a career combining corporate finance and entrepreneurial business skills. His opening statement was quite unequivocal: 'I have been extremely lucky'. I was determined to find out if there was any magic attached to his luck or if we could accommodate it into our structure.

Richard believes that he was lucky in his upbringing, encouraged by his parents to find the right career path and nudged gently into accountancy, where he was lucky enough to be with the right kind of boss who allowed him to take on more responsibilities than he might have expected. His happy marriage was a lucky event; Richard jokingly refers to it as 'an arranged marriage' because he was introduced to his wife Susie by his parents. He claims that his happy marriage and family life have been the bedrock of his career and have stopped him from being a workaholic.

Richard has a belief that people beat a path to his door and that this is a consequence of luck. Closer examination would seem to indicate that he had a great skill with people, getting the best out of them and making the right kind of business relationship.

He cites a time when the buyer for a key customer was leaving, putting at risk 50% of Richard's turnover. The relationship with the new buyer was critical to the business going forward. 'Fortunately,' said Richard, 'we got on famously and it worked brilliantly.' Luck? Nothing to do, then, with Richard's determination to make things work, or his ability to get on with people?

Richard has even been lucky in his holidays, inadvertently making key business contacts when he has been away skiing. Hold on, don't we think this is one of the key indicators of luck – the ability to meet other people and forge meaningful relationships? You have to be 'in to win', and it would seem that Richard is in.

He believes that the twenty-first century will require people to start valuing relationships again, not only through building strong teams in the business but also by valuing customers, suppliers and shareholders. Spoken like a true networker who knows that relationships underpin everything.

I am beginning to get slightly unnerved by all of this good luck, so I ask Richard if he is a risk-taker. He laughs with incredulity. An accountant? A chief executive? Oh no, he does not take risks. We then went on to discuss the acquisition of David S. Smith and what he had to do to gain control. It would seem that he had to take out a large mortgage and put a significant part of his own assets at risk in order to make the deal work.

At that time he had two small children and Susie was expecting their third child, so he was quite economical with the truth of what he had to risk personally to make the deal work. 'Ah-ha, one to me there', I thought to myself. An ambitious person who is prepared to risk all when he has to but doesn't recognise it as a risk – it was just what he had to do to get what he wanted.

I mentally mark him down as a 6 on the risk scale. I know I am right when his advice for today's entrepreneur is to be bold, to go out there, to use a professional background and use it to advantage.

Overwhelmingly, I find that Richard is someone who accepts responsibility for where he is in life. He has a plan for his life and clearly established goals. Business inevitably brings with it highs and lows, and it is interesting to see that Richard never blames anyone for when things go wrong. He tells me that he is an optimistic person and always thought that he could win the day.

As I walk out, I reflect on Richard Brewster – a lucky man who knows the skills and behaviours needed to attract luck into life. He does all of these things at an intuitive level so will probably still argue that it is just a matter of luck …

Stick-Ability

> 'Every worthwhile accomplishment, big or little,
> has its stages of drudgery and triumph, a beginning,
> a struggle and a victory.' – Mahatma Gandhi

Stick-Ability is about perseverance, tenacity and following things through – even when the odds are against you. It is about finishing off what you start.

Result? Achieving goals no-one else thought possible.

Stick-Ability and what it means for you

Lucky people stick at things!

Lucky people are people who don't give up! They are the ones who believe in finishing off what they have started and are undeterred by obstacles in their path. Not for them the sudden enthusiasms that evaporate after a few days or weeks;

If you want to know more about Stick-Ability, read Case Studies 1 (page 192) and 8 (page 228)

lucky people focus on what they want and what they need to do to get there. When problems occur, they find answers. When their plans are disrupted, they create new ones. They have the tenacity to see things through.

Seeing things through is a common thread with people who seem to get it right in life, whereas flighty will-o'-the-wisps move on before ideas turn into a working reality. Not every-one can turn themselves into this model of completed projects; those who don't should consider joining those people who always finish the crossword, never abandon a book halfway through and always paint the last bit of the skirting board in the spare bedroom.

We have discovered that all of our successful entrepre-neurs have stuck at things when others would have given up. Tenacity, stubbornness and a willingness to see things through are the hallmark of those who get where they want to be. They give up the short-term gain to have the long-term rewards. They recognise that they might have to sacrifice things along the way but their determination to succeed out-strips everything else. As Samuel Johnson said, 'great works are performed not by strength but by perseverance'.

Fabulous determination – or stubbornness?

But how do you tell the difference between, on the one hand, the perspicacity and inspirational entrepreneurial thinking of someone who goes after their dream, and on the other, wrong-headed stubbornness that may lead to some kind of personal disaster? How do you know the difference between the route that takes you to the debtor's prison and the one that buys you a house on millionaire's row?

Twenty-twenty hindsight would work marvellously when you are assessing whether you should persevere with your plans, your projects or your dreams. If you stick at it and you hit the jackpot, you are admired for your judgement and your skills. If you don't pull it off, you will have people telling you that you have thrown good money after bad, and that you should have got yourself a proper job and settled for less. Unfortunately we don't have a crystal ball.

Stick-Ability needs to work alongside many of the other luck indicators in this book. All seven indicators of luck work together, but perhaps only Stick-Ability needs to be supported by one or more of the other indicators if you are to be considered lucky or successful. Many people work very hard and stick at something long after others give up, but are not successful because they have not got the self-awareness of high Percept-Ability. Alternatively, they perhaps have low Risk-Ability and are not open to the ideas and views of others – they work in a vacuum.

When epileptic ex-builder Andrew Halsey set off in an attempt to row the Pacific Ocean single-handed, disaster awaited him. His starting point in Peru was 8,108 miles from his destination in Brisbane, Australia.

After 72 gruelling days at sea, fighting strong winds and currents, he was still exactly 8,108 miles away! He broke the record for travelling the least distance in the most time – not quite the record he was hoping for. And this was his second attempt. He said, in the midst of his difficulties, 'Don't worry – I am going to keep going, I can sit out here for years'.

In the event, he had four epileptic seizures, almost starved to death and had to be rescued. You have to admire his Stick-Ability but question his judgement and Person-Ability.

Most people know that James Dyson was the inventor of a revolutionary bag-less vacuum cleaner. What many people do not know is that it took him five years and 5127 proto-types before he was able to put his first finished product on the market. He stuck to his vision despite many setbacks, including near-bankruptcy

Dyson is now a household name and James Dyson is one of Britain's top 50 richest men His story calls to mind that of David and Goliath, with James taking on the mighty Hoover and vanquishing them in their marketplace. The odds were against it happening but he risked all and persevered stubbornly to achieve a dream.

So what's the answer?

There is no single answer to knowing whether something is worth sticking at or if you are flogging a dead horse, but two things are essential. Firstly, you need to have the level of awareness about your own skills and capabilities that will enable you to assess the chances of success. The second is to be clear about what you want: 'if you don't know where you are going, how do you know when you have arrived?', as the saying goes. Chapter 6, on Percept-Ability, is the right place to discover the secret of successful goal setting.

Martha Lane Fox was one of the early pioneers in the burgeoning dotcom industry and co-founder of lastminute.com. Days after floating her company on the Stock Exchange, she was a multi-millionaire. Within a year, however, her company collapsed and very nearly went bust. So many investors lost money that she was named the most hated woman in Britain.

Did she throw in the towel? No. She stuck with her company and set about rebuilding it. Today, lastminute.com is again one of the leaders in e-tailing. Interestingly, it is apparent that along with her high Stick-Ability, Martha Lane Fox has also demonstrated the value of both high Sense-Ability and high Risk-Ability. She claims that the best advice she was ever given was to 'think big and act fast'.* She is also quoted as saying you should 'get on with things as soon as you get that earth-shattering idea. Taking risks is a good thing if you feel like it. People should be prepared to go with their gut instinct if they feel it is the right thing to do.'

No-one can tell you whether you are right or wrong if you choose to stick at something, stubbornly determined to get to where you want to be. Equally, no-one can tell you that you are wrong if you decided to throw the towel in. Strong Stick-Ability is about choice: choosing when to stop doing something, rather than abandoning it or letting it drift, so it loses momentum and stops of its own volition. On the other hand, it is also about *choosing* to continue rather than going at something out of habit.

Test your Stick-Ability out!

Do you have any of the following in your life?

- ❖ Gym membership (seldom used);
- ❖ Tennis rackets (bent);
- ❖ Golf clubs (brand new);
- ❖ Badminton rackets (somewhere or other);
- ❖ Cricket bats (slightly mildewed);
- ❖ Musical instruments (unplayed);
- ❖ Fishing rods (dusty);
- ❖ Bicycles (rusty);

---

* From Hoberman, as reported in *Media Guardian*, 25 March 2002

- Windsurfer (in bits);
- Computer games (still in box);
- Keep-fit equipment (the instructions are somewhere);
- Linguaphone tapes or CDs (still in box);
- Books (unread);
- Paints, watercolour sets (brand new);
- Cookery books (on the shelf);
- Black & Decker tool sets (look very nice);
- Cans of emulsion paint (unopened);
- Application forms for planning permission (half filled in);
- Journal and diaries (blank);
- Job application forms (not filled in); or
- Distance learning or study courses (abandoned).

How well did you do?

Please feel free here to add in your own guilty secrets. Funny, isn't it, that we didn't add unfinished bottles of wine, holidays abandoned halfway through or unopened boxes of chocolates?

Think about it – how different would your life be now if you had persevered with any one of those half-finished items? You might be a talented linguist in a better job, a competent sportsperson, have more friends, be more interesting to talk to, be more creative or simply have discovered the pleasure of opening up a new side of your personality.

Meredith Belbin carried out nine years of experiments into management teams at Henley Management College and developed the Team Role Type Theory. In his book *Management Teams: Why They Succeed Or Fail*, he says that in every team there is a need for a completer-finisher, the person who has the capacity for follow-through, perfectionism and delivering on time. Completer-finishers are unlikely to start anything that they cannot finish. In management, they excel by meeting the high standards to which they aspire and by their concern for precision, attention to detail and follow-through. Apparently, only 3% of the management population has the capacity to finish things off.

The key issue for lucky people is to have judgement, skill and self-awareness, combined with the will to take a risk or to know when to persevere in the face of uncertainty and the disapproval of others.

The other side of this coin is to recognise when you are going down a blind alley. Lucky people often hear others saying, 'I had that idea but didn't bother doing anything about it'. Lucky people have the idea and then follow through, overcoming barriers, scepticism, perceived wisdom, anguish, self-doubt and cash shortfalls in order to achieve their goal.

A head-hunter of our acquaintance began her search career as a researcher. She loathed every second of her work but stuck at it because it was the only job she could get and she needed the money. She chose to stick at it because she knew she had to generate income. She was in the position for two years, enduring a difficult and unrewarding job but learning many skills along the way. She also learnt that she could do more than she realised. As a result of this testing 'apprenticeship', she went on to build a significant business that was sold for millions.

Perseverance brings with it the last laugh and remember: those who laugh last, laugh longest. Lucky people laugh a lot! Our successful and 'lucky' people unanimously agree that a key factor of their success was persevering when others

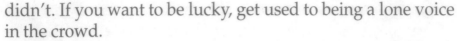

didn't. If you want to be lucky, get used to being a lone voice in the crowd.

There is no getting away from it: Stick-Ability means hard work, long hours and a commitment that is second to none. 'The harder I work, the luckier I get' is a truism difficult to deny.

Free flowing or drifting?

When you have a goal and you are clear about what you want things become easier. You stick at them because you like them, they provide purpose in your life, you can measure your progress towards your goal and you enjoy what you do. You are free flowing – *and free flowing is better than drifting*.

Drifting is reactive, whereas moving purposefully towards a goal is a choice. What most successful people have discovered is that it is as important *not* to do something as it is to do it. The default position in our lives is where we end up by failing to take a position or to make a positive choice. As a friend of ours is fond of saying, 'When you come to the fork in the road – take it!'

Stick-Ability and relationships

Long-term friendships and relationships don't just happen of their own accord: you have to work at them and be prepared to make the effort to keep in touch with others. A card at Christmas is just not enough. Consider how important it might be to maintain contact, even if they have not returned your call, or sent you a birthday or Christmas card, or sent you an invitation to a celebration. It is a lot easier to cut someone out of your life than to invite them in. Perhaps we should fight any inclination to assume the worst about others, so sticking with friendships may require a shift in attitude: 'a person is doing just the best they can'.

Stick–Ability in sport and business

Business has woken up to the fact that it has a lot to learn from the sporting world. Athletes and sports people perform at their best when they are, as they describe it, 'in the zone'. They are clear about their goals, they have stuck at their training, they believe in themselves and they visualise success.

It is a well-known fact that visualisation improves performance, as well as constant practice. The winning mindset is inextricably linked with the finishing post, whatever that might be. The route to it started with establishing what the goal was, the behaviour to reach it verged almost on the obsessive and the satisfaction of achievement was enhanced by knowing that it was meant to happen.

Everyone knows that Jonny Wilkinson, the hero of the 2003 Rugby World Cup, persevered day in, day out – even on Boxing Day – to perfect his drop-kick. A large part of the successful sportsman's strategy is to visualise that moment of success. The roar of the crowd, the feeling of elation, the celebratory thumping on the back from team-mates and the sight of thousands of people on their feet with the hands in the air is the inspiration underpinning the routine of solitary practice.

The net result of not choosing is that we lose control, we feel under stress and we use words like 'if only', 'I ought to' or 'I should have'. Remember, one of the choices always open to you is to change your goal and to decide not to continue down the path you had previously established. Actively choosing whether to do something can be very liberating.

Create your own success: create Stick-Ability

What will happen if you don't have Stick-Ability?

Stick-Ability is not just about sticking at things once you have started; it is also about starting something even though you can't see the immediate benefit. This could be a job opportunity that you let pass by because it is not the ideal one and is not the instant perfect position.

If you don't have Stick-Ability, you will have fewer opportunities because you reject them out of hand. Sometimes you have to serve an apprenticeship in learning, experience, relationships, patience and skills in order to have the foundation stones necessary for that lucky break.

People who give up before the finishing line tend to look at others and say 'I could have done that. They were just luckier than me.' Serial disappointment is likely to be their lot. Life for them will be full of 'if onlys'.

What won't happen if you don't have Stick-Ability?

If you are someone who keeps giving up, you will never know what you were capable of achieving. That final stretch of overcoming seemingly impossible obstacles was never one you managed, so who knows just how good you are? You won't have put your ideas to the test, you won't have fulfilled your true potential and your life will be full of 'might have beens'. You will miss the satisfaction of seeing something through from start to finish.

Alternatively, on the plus side, it could well be that you don't run the risk of wasting your time on projects that are doomed to failure. The choice is yours.

What won't happen if you do have Stick-Ability?

People who do have Stick-Ability will not be put off from achieving their goals by setbacks, criticism, problems or general difficulties. They won't settle for second best; they will determinedly work their way through to a solution. They won't have the guilt of leaving projects half-finished.

What will happen if you do have Stick-Ability?

Lucky people stick at things and see things through to the finish. Lucky people live their dreams, pursuing their goals in the knowledge that they will get there. Other people will look at them with admiration, knowing that they are completer-finishers who always deliver what they promise.

People with Stick-Ability know what it is to have the satisfaction of a job well done, despite obstacles encountered along the way. Their confidence will be greater than most people because they keep on achieving when others said they couldn't. This fulfilment is more likely to bring happiness and satisfaction.

Remember: Stick-Ability helps you to make the impossible possible.

Make life go your way

The effects of having or not having Stick-Ability are shown in Table 2.1.

Table 2.1 *Make life go your way*

What will happen if you do have Stick-Ability?	What will happen if you don't have Stick-Ability?
You will see things through to the finish	You will miss lots of chances and opportunities
You will finish off what you start	You will suffer the stress generated by a pile of unfinished tasks
You will achieve things that others said were impossible	You will have a graveyard of unused golf clubs, sports equipment, guitars, half-read books, underused gym membership, half-finished study courses and abandoned night classes
You will get the satisfaction of a job well done	
People will have confidence in your ability to deliver	
You will continue to pursue your goals in the knowledge that you will get there	
You will live your dreams	You will look back with regret at things you could have done
	You will miss the success that comes from seeing things through from start to finish
What won't happen if you don't have Stick-Ability?	**What won't happen if you do have Stick-Ability?**
You won't know what you were capable of achieving	You won't be deterred by obstacles
You won't have put your ideas to the test	You won't have the guilt from abandoned projects
You won't have fulfilled your true potential	You won't settle for the average or the easiest option

Brilliant Ideas for using Stick-Ability to increase your luck

Consider different options

Remember that if you continue to do things the same way, you will always get the same result. Consider altering your mindset, opening up to other possibilities and trying out different ways to achieve your goals.

For example, you could make some different assumptions about what you:

❖ can/can't do;
❖ like/dislike; and
❖ want/don't want.

Make a choice

Get accustomed to asking yourself 'Do I choose to do this or choose not to?', as well as weighing things up properly rather than letting things slip by.

Pick up an enthusiasm

Choose one item from the graveyard of unused hobbies or activities that you have accumulated and follow it through.

Make a list

Make a list of your unfinished tasks and choose which ones you will see through to completion. For each completed task, tick the box and feel the satisfaction.

Reward yourself

Promise yourself a reward for a completed task that you didn't really want to do. Make sure you give yourself that reward.

Stand on the shoulders of giants

Most of our behaviours are acquired by imitating others. Other people's language style, vocabulary, attitudes and even beliefs can unconsciously rub off onto us.

As well as doing it naturally and unconsciously, we can change the way we do things by observing what works for others and trying those behaviours on to see what they feel like.

Think of someone you know who is a lucky person and who has demonstrated tenacity and perseverance. You might not like everything about them, but you admire their achievements.

Study them to find out what they do in terms of perseverance and Stick-Ability to help them achieve their goals. Adapt their way of doing things so that it feels right for you and see what a difference it makes.

Decision time

Ask yourself what is important for you in your:

* life;
* career;
* relationships;
* financial status;
* health;

- ❖ leisure;
- ❖ positions; and
- ❖ personal development.

Choose the headings that matter to you and add others if necessary. For each one, write a goal using the following guidelines:

Step 1: make it SMART

- ❖ S – Simple: don't make it too wordy or complex.
- ❖ M – Meaningful to you: this needs to be something you really want, not what someone else wants for you.
- ❖ A – As if now: write your goal in the present tense, as if it is already happening; for example, 'I am a fluent French speaker' or 'I drive a BMW'.
- ❖ R – Realistic: use your judgement to determine how ambitious you want to be.
- ❖ T – Towards what you want: use language that will ensure that you are going towards what you want, not what you don't want; for example, say 'I want to pass my exams' rather than 'I don't want to fail my exams'.

Step 2: paint the picture

Make your goal real and appealing by seeing it in your mind's eye, with as many details as you can provide. For example, if you want a house in Provence, picture your ideal home and garden. How many rooms does it have? What colours are the shutters at the windows? Do you hear the noise of your neighbours, or just birds singing and the chirping of the cicadas? See yourself and your family enjoying the house and garden.

If you want a BMW, see it on your drive. What colour is it? How many doors does it have? What colour is the interior trim? Hear the noise of the engine when you start it up. See yourself driving it.

Step 3: keep your picture handy

Capture that picture as though it were a photograph or a video. Keep it at the forefront of your mind and check it out daily. Adjust the picture as if it were on your television set so that the colours and sound are just how you prefer them. Keep this picture compelling so that action towards it becomes almost automatic.

Step 4: do something now!

Write down the first step towards achieving your goal and do it within 24 hours.

Step 5: back to step 3

The success of this technique is being determined enough to keep your mental picture at the front of your mind and revisit it regularly. For most people this is the hard part, so what can you do when you find yourself on the verge of giving up?

- ❖ Revisit your goal. Check that you still really want it, determine what will happen if you don't get it and decide if you are ready to pay that price.
- ❖ Go into the future and look back at where you are today. Feel what it is like to have given up at this stage. Now look back and feel the difference between that and the feeling of having achieved it.
- ❖ Choose a friend who has wisdom and judgement. Confide in them and ask their opinion, then decide whether you choose to take their advice or not.

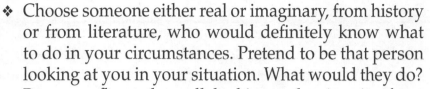

❖ Choose someone either real or imaginary, from history or from literature, who would definitely know what to do in your circumstances. Pretend to be that person looking at you in your situation. What would they do?

❖ Become a fly on the wall, looking at the situation from another angle or from a distance. Look at the whole picture, past, present and future. Gain the benefits of this new perspective.

❖ Remember a time when you stuck at something against all odds and it really worked. Recapture the feeling of that situation and how glad you were that you did not give up.

Start continue stop

You can try a quick test on your level of Stick-Ability by asking yourself which of the following you find most difficult:

❖ starting things;
❖ continuing things; or
❖ stopping things.

Let's look at these in reverse order.

Stopping things

If you find stopping things hardest, you are likely to be determined and good at persevering. Your challenge will be to know the difference between something that has just become a habit and something that you really want to do. You may even end up never finishing something. Try asking yourself, 'Why am I continuing to do this?' If you have a good reason, then carry on. If you don't, you should reconsider your options.

Continuing things

If you find continuing things hardest, then Stick-Ability might be a problem for you. Ask yourself, 'What would be some good reasons for continuing to stick at this?' If you can find some, this might motivate you and make it easier for you to follow something through to the finish. If you *can't* find any good reasons, then make a decision and actively *choose* not to carry on rather than simply giving up.

Starting things

Of course, if you find starting things the hardest, this may have a connection to low Risk-Ability and the desire to stay in the same place rather than wanting to try out new and different things. Remember that really lucky people have high scores in most, if not all, of the Luck Indicators.

Brilliant Ideas pushed to the outer limits

Rocks in the jar

When you find you are ready to give up on something, you may find it is because it does not match your values. Why is this? Because the stronger the value, the stronger the motivation. A lack of motivation frequently means that what you are doing is not sufficiently important to you.

Consider the story of the rocks in the jar.

A teacher was standing in front of students and sensed that he had lost their attention. He produced from a cupboard a large, open-necked jar and set on the table in front of the class. He then produced about ten rocks the size of an orange and carefully placed them, one at a time, into the jar. When the jar was filled to the top and no more rocks would fit inside, he asked the students, 'Is the jar full?' They all said that it was.

Next, he produced a container full of gravel. He carefully poured the gravel through the rocks until he could fit no more in. 'Is the jar full now?' he asked. By this time the class was paying attention and began to understand what the teacher was getting at. 'Probably not,' one of them answered.

The teacher smiled and produced a bag of sand that he carefully trickled into the jar so that it went into all the spaces left between the rocks and the gravel. Again, he asked, 'Is the jar full?' By this time the class was certain that it was not. He took a pitcher of water and began to pour it in until the jar was filled to the brim.

The point of this story is to recognise what the 'big rocks' in your life are. You may want to include your children, your family, your career, your personal development, your dreams, a worthy cause, coaching or mentoring others, doing things that you love, time for yourself, your health or your partner. Remember to put these big rocks in first, or you'll never get them in at all. If you start off with the gravel or sand, you'll fill your life worrying about little things that don't really matter and you'll never have the time you need to spend on the big, important things.

Begin at the end

If you find sticking to a project hard work and become discouraged, use the following method to re-motivate yourself.

Picture the outcome you are working toward as if it is on a television screen. The important thing is to see yourself in the picture. For example, if you are planning the fête for the local resident's association, imagine a successful day and see yourself at the end of it being congratulated on such a well-organised and successful event. This small exercise may seem simple but it is very powerful – try it! It will give you the inspiration to continue.

Relax!

This one may seem a little odd, but sometimes working too hard can demoralise you and stop you from sticking at things. Mental and physical exhaustion can be barriers to getting things done.

While there is a bit of truth in the cliché 'the harder I work the luckier I get', it is not the whole truth. Hard work is a key component of lucky breaks. It is easy to forget that it's also important sometimes to work *less* hard.

Here we have a good example of a powerful paradox: you must work hard to achieve success but you must relax and allow things to develop of their own accord.

The most successful people, however, are often those who are also able to relax physically and therefore mentally.

Somehow the relaxation state seems to slow down the metabolism in a way that provides more energy than sleep. Research has shown that 20 minutes of relaxation can provide up to four hours of mental alertness. Not bad for an investment of time!

There are many ways to relax and many relaxation products on the market such as audio tapes, videos and DVDs. It's worth trying a few out until you find the one that works best for you.

So what's stopping you from sticking at things?

Luck Master 3: Stuart Greenwood

Stuart is Chief Executive of B&M Retail in Blackpool, a chain of shops he bought into after the sale of the Greeting Cards Group in 1998. His route to this entrepreneurial success has not been straightforward, and I wanted to find out how he had picked himself up after he left a PLC and saw one paper fortune melt in front of his eyes. He made and lost millions in the early 1990s, and has gone on to win it all back again. Lesser people would have settled for what they could get – but not Stuart.

When he was 18, his destiny was to be a geography teacher. He had accepted a place at university and took a gap year when he began to question his life. One day in 1966 he read the *Sunday Times* and saw that 'these accountants seem to do all right' – and the course of his business life was set. Geography was forgotten and he accepted articles to train as an accountant.

By 1987, his career had progressed to the point where he was the Finance Director of a high-profile listed company. Life was going well. However, a chance meeting in 1990 led to discussions that meant he moved to a lower-profile yet fast-growing business a year later. 'Why on earth did you take a risk like that?' I asked. His reply was that 'it didn't feel like a risk'. This is something we have seen before. Like many other 'lucky', successful people, he takes risks that others wouldn't but often only because he does not always recognise a risk when he sees it.

The gamble paid off for a while, but then disaster struck and he was outside the PLC, having to start again from scratch. This time his strong network stood him in good stead and new opportunities arose. Rather than looking for a job, Stuart took control of his own life and went out to acquire a business with his business partner. He was looking for 'little business shooting stars' and acquired a card group consisting of 11 shops. Stuart says modestly that 'we did well', having built up a business in a sector he knew nothing about from 11 shops operating at break-even point to a chain of 211 that was sold for £29.5 million to Clinton Cards. Not satisfied with that, he is doing it all again with B&M Retail.

'Luck?' asks Stuart. 'It can drift across your path – then you have to seize it and make it work.' How did he do it? It is easy to see the hard work, tenacity and strong business network, underpinned by self-belief and an ability to take risks. He speaks with animation of the time when he and his board brought a business out of receivership at the High Court in London. They had done practically no due diligence, yet borrowed £5 million and gave an undertaking to pay creditors within 30 days. He took the risk because he knew they could do it and make it work. Stuart has that positive view of life derived from the Percept-Ability that we applaud in lucky people.

Stuart uses all of his Percept-Ability to expect the best in a situation and uses all of his Control-Ability to accept responsibility when things go wrong. Stuart believes that success comes to those who are bright, quick-witted and switched on, but thinks they also have to be doggedly determined. When he describes his time with the Greeting Store Group, he says that he 'scratched at it and scratched at it and hung in and hung in'. Success does not come to those who give up easily. Opportunities came along for Stuart and he says that 'we had the vision and we saw the opportunity. Then the opportunity turned out to be much bigger than we envisaged, but you just have to go for it.' Stuart went for it, worked at it and says he will do it all again with B&M Retail.

And after that? He still wants to start something from scratch, as he thinks that is the hallmark of the true entrepreneur. From where I am sitting, it looks as though he has all of the qualities we have seen in really lucky people …

3

Risk–Ability

'It's kind of fun to do the impossible.' – Walt Disney

Risk-Ability is the confidence to take a chance rather than plumping for the safe bet, as well as having an open mindset and a willingness to explore and experiment with new ways of thinking and doing things.
Result? More lucky opportunities.

Risk–Ability and what it means for you

What do you think of when you talk about risk and what does risk mean for you?

The answer you give to this question will help determine your attitude to risk and define where you sit on the Richter scale of risk. If your instant response is to think of the potential downside of a big decision, or if you experience fear when fac-

---

If you want to know more about Risk-Ability, read Case Studies 1 (page 192), 2 (page 199), 3 (page 203), 5 (page 213) and 6 (page 218)

ing that decision rather than the adrenaline rush of excitement, then your place on the Risk-Ability scale is likely to be low.

On the other hand, if you love the buzz you get from taking challenging decisions when the outcome is uncertain, underpinned by confidence in your ability to make things happen, then you are likely to be a top scorer on the Risk-Ability scale.

Risk is often associated with financial matters and their consequences but it is something that affects every area of our lives if we choose to let it. Risk is *relative*. Some people see danger lurking around every corner, whereas others are blissfully unaware. For some people, debt is the nagging worry about last week's unpaid newspaper bill. For others, large borrowings, big mortgages or heavy credit card bills are not an area for concern.

The real power of risk is that it takes you beyond your known horizons and puts new possibilities before you. You can win or lose when you venture into the world of risk; a comfort zone will be a thing of the past, since you will be doing things differently and therefore getting different results.

Where does high risk stop and start for you?

For some of us, 'high risk' would be bungee jumping at Victoria Falls, signing a personal guarantee against a business, marrying someone you have only known for two days or using venture capital to fund a management buyout. Some of us prefer the certainty and comfort of our steady, predictable and controlled existence: whether that is a fur-lined rut or an uncomfortable bed of nails, taking risks would bring with it uncertainty, lack of control and the fear that life could go badly wrong.

Others welcome change and need to have in their lives some unpredictability – the challenge of getting out of their comfort zone and the opportunity to do things differently.

Neither route is right or wrong, yet this fundamental difference in attitude to risk will radically change your luck. All the people interviewed for this book were crystal clear about their attitude to risk and where they lay on this scale. They knew what they would do and what they would not.

John Miller, former Chief Executive of the Halifax Building Society, believes that a successful entrepreneur is someone who is oblivious to the risks that he is running. An entrepreneur, according to John, is someone who is likely to say 'Don't confuse me with facts'. All of our interviewees agreed that it is action that counts and they like to go with the Nike slogan – 'just do it'. They may not always have all of the facts at their fingertips, but they do get on and do it.

People who filled in the Luck Questionnaire on our website **www.switchtosuccess.co.uk** showed themselves generally to be a risk-taking bunch of people. Seventy per cent were more likely to take a chance than not. It would seem that we all believe that we are ready and willing to go for it if it crosses our path. Are we really?

Here's a quiz for you:

Question: Five frogs are sitting on a log. Four of them decide to jump in. How many are left on the log?

Answer: It could be one, two, three, four or five, because there is another step after 'decision' called 'action'. Four of them decided to jump off but we don't know if they did it or not.

We know a chief executive of a nationwide chain of his own supermarkets who believes that most people just talk a good game. He thinks that the critical difference between him and

69

others is that whereas other people just talk, he just gets on and does things.

A critical crossroads for his business was the day when the opportunity arose to buy out his largest competitor. He could have stayed where he was with a well-run, profitable business that was within his control. Instead, he decided to take the high-risk route, relying on his business skills and his confidence in his ability to make the deal work. He raised money via venture capitalists, recognising that he was putting his existing highly profitable business at risk but believing that he would make it work and become even more successful. And it did.

This chief executive belongs to the minority of people that puts into action what most people only talk about. Maybe, as he points out, one of the factors that encouraged him to take the risk and get on with it was that he was quite naïve, not recognising what it would cost him to build this dream or what he might have to lose in terms of lifestyle in order to make it work. Risk combined with perseverance – what a combination!

Companies also have different attitudes to risk, which reflects what happens at a personal level.

When BEA and BOAC merged to form British Airways, there was a huge clash of cultures based on attitude to risk. Both organisations were in a highly regulated environment. The people in BEA looked at the regulations, and the philosophy was if it didn't say you couldn't do it, then it was OK to go ahead and do it. Perhaps they went by the old adage that it is better to ask for forgiveness than permission.

The people in BOAC took a different view – if the regulation didn't specifically allow something, they assumed it couldn't be done. Both were looking at the same regulations with very different outcomes. One was risk-averse and the other was more open to risk.

The Great British Dream seems to have moved on from owning your own home to owning your own home abroad. Statistics show that at least one million people own a property in France, with at least 300,000 of them living, working and raising their children there. So many people are seduced by the thought of the rural idyll, the warm weather and the dream of the 'good life', and they risk it all by selling up and moving on.

What helps them to do it? Enthusiasm, confidence in their abilities to overcome any problems and the thought of that elusively idyllic lifestyle. We all know from the reality television programmes that they hit financial problems, language barriers, local bureaucracy, illness, unreliable builders and plumbers – yet most of them make it work.

They took a risk in pursuit of their goal and, once committed, they had to get on with it. There are probably a million more who think longingly of the olive groves and lavender fields but who are not prepared to risk what they have for what they think could be.

Luck Master 4: David Toon

David Toon, a main board director of Johnson Service Group PLC, talked to me about how to bring discipline and structure to business, thus eliminating the need to rely on a stroke of luck. When David comes into the room, he makes an instant impression, since he is tall and emanates pace and energy. I think the only acknowledgement he had for luck was that he thinks that his sheer physical size has always worked well for him. David has always been in a hurry, keen to get results and impatient with bureaucracy and meaningless systems. He does not like to be tied down or constrained by the limiting factors of needless close scrutiny; give David impossible targets and a free rein, and he will get there seemingly effortlessly.

David believes that a great impetus for his own success has been that he has always had great bosses. Underpinning business success and luck, for him, is the strength of a team. He has a high level of self-awareness, so when he is building a management team he makes sure that he brings in people who have the skills that he lacks. He stays in touch with people, not letting people he values drop out of his life. I asked him if he was good networker and he winced imperceptibly. David does not go in for socialising, so you might think that he is low on Socia-Ability. The truth, however, is that he excels at maintaining relationships in his life but not with the goal of self-promotion. His form of networking revolves around the needs of the business and David's genuine wish to maintain friendships rather than the social interaction fuelled by cynical self-interest. This gives us a new take on Socia-Ability – strong relationships, actively nurtured, giving a solid platform in life.

Life, according to David, is a risk. It happens all the time. Markets change, customers change, products change. David has worked for years in a sector where prices have fallen every year and he has built a business by accepting the problem and facing it. The real issue for David with regards to risk is getting to grips with the potential difficulties and then deciding what to make of them. He sees opportunities rather than risks. He does not believe in right or wrong answers; the solution lies in how you deal with the consequences of decisions. The real danger, David believes, is allowing yourself to be restricted by your fears rather than belief in your ability to deliver results, no matter how good or bad the initial decision was.

David's greatest strength would seem to be his ability to see the positives in every situation. He cites the time very early on in his career when he was made redundant. He did not take it personally; he preferred to see it as an opportunity and 'just moved on'. He likes to be in charge of his own destiny. He looks forward, not back, and believes that he does not have a care in the world. He has a job that he loves, full of challenges and the pressure to deliver results. Money is a part of his definition of success, but not a part to be over-estimated: it is a symptom of success rather than success itself. He does not seem to have clear goals and ambitions, apart from the need to enjoy what he is doing and to be tested. He said, 'Something will come along and I will think, "That's what I want to do", and go ahead and do it.' Self-belief, confidence, optimism and positive thinking, combined with a refusal to accept the fear of a risk – that's the contribution that David makes to his business and that's why he enjoys the success of a lucky person.

Create your own success: create Risk-Ability

What will happen if you don't have Risk-Ability?

Taking risks is not for everybody, so let's analyse the consequences if we decide that risk-taking is not for us.

You'll stay with the tried and tested methods. One definition of insanity is continuing to repeat the same behaviour and expect different results. Taking risks means trying out new things and new behaviours.

Tried and tested methods are fine if you are happy with the way your life is running. How many people, though, do you hear complaining about their situation but are not prepared to do something different in order to change it? Typically, they consider themselves to be unlucky in their relationships, jobs or social situation, but are not prepared to take a risk to change it.

The net result of this is that where you are is where you are always likely to be, and you will hold on to what you have. Your life is likely to be more predictable, your path is likely to be steady and measured, and with no shocks. You are likely to take into account rules, regulations and restrictions when they do not actually exist.

If this is how you want to live your life, that is fine. However, if you feel that you want to be more, have more and do more, then you need to consider raising the level of risk in your life.

Before you do this, consider what won't happen if you don't have the ability to take risks. One thing's certain – you won't win a lot or lose a lot. 'Average' will be a big word in your life. You won't experience the full potential of life. You won't experience great riches but you won't experience great poverty either. There are always people who are willing to point to the downside of any situation. It takes a lot of confidence and courage to fly in the face of conventional wisdom and knowledge.

If Christopher Columbus had accepted conventional wisdom that the world was flat, America would not have been discovered when it was.

An entrepreneurial managing director of our acquaintance states openly that he would rather reward spectacular failure than employ people who did nothing. People always say that they learn more from their failures than their successes. These only come about through risk-taking. *Taking risks increases your openness to luck.*

What won't happen if you don't have Risk-Ability?

Many people are very hesitant about taking risks and they will never know whether they were right or wrong because they won't know what they have missed out on. For some people this is a safe and reassuring place to be, because it minimises new situations, change and the opportunities for things to go wrong. Equally, those who don't take risks don't reap large rewards.

What won't happen if you do have Risk-Ability?

One thing to recognise if you like taking risks is that you may not see potential problems. Sometimes this is an advantage if the problems can be overcome. At other times, it can explain why many entrepreneurs go bankrupt more than once.

The prisons of Britain are full of people who took risks but didn't take the downside into account. Driving licences are full of penalty points because people take a chance that they won't get caught. People who are caught speeding often feel they have been unlucky rather than having been caught when taking an unacceptable risk. Risk evaluation needs to be accompanied by experience, intelligence, data and judgement.

You are also less likely to have regrets about lost opportunities if you take chances along the way. There is a huge amount of research conducted among people in their latter years. When asked about what they regretted about their lives, the consistent pattern emerged that they did not regret past actions, whether successful or not. Their main regrets were the opportunities in life that they did *not* take because they were afraid of the risk.

You only have to go to the pub to hear people talking about lost chances. Are you one of those?

What will happen if you do have Risk-Ability?

Risks bring with them the chance of greater rewards or greater loss. By being prepared to open your mind, your comfort zone will expand and you will feel at ease in a greater variety of situations more often.

High self-confidence and self-belief generally lead to a readiness to take more risks than most people. Self-confident people expose themselves to the possibility of failure all the time. As their successes stack up, so does their confidence – and so their good luck increases. Failures are either not recognised as such or are used as a platform for learning or trying something different.

Make life go your way

The effects of having or not having Risk-Ability are shown in Table 3.1.

Lucky people take risks. They're the ones who, in our frogs puzzle (see above), have jumped in the pond. The safest option is to stay on the log with the companionship of your fellow frogs.

Lucky people are prepared for the consequences of their actions. They know that what they do may not work. They know that they increase their chances of success by experimenting. Lucky people who take risks say:

- ❖ 'It's always worth a try.'
- ❖ 'What's the worst thing that can happen?'
- ❖ 'You've got to be in to win.'
- ❖ 'That sounds exciting.'
- ❖ 'High risk, high reward.'
- ❖ 'I bet I can make that work.'
- ❖ 'Nothing ventured, nothing gained.'

Table 3.1 *Make life go your way*

What will happen if you do have Risk-Ability?	What will happen if you don't have Risk-Ability?
You will be thinking like an entrepreneur	You'll stay with the tried and tested methods
You will increase the chances of success in whatever you tackle	Where you are is where you are always likely to be
You will be experimental in your outlook	You'll hold onto what you have
You will challenge perceived wisdom	Your life is likely to be more predictable
You will be looked on as a path-finder	Your path is likely to be steady, measured and even – with no shocks
You will know you have the skills to achieve your goals	You'll see the downside of the risk more than the upside
You'll see the upside of the risk more than the downside	Your life will be more constricted
You will look for new and imaginative ways to do things	

What won't happen if you don't have Risk-Ability?	What won't happen if you do have Risk-Ability?
You won't have the nerve to stand up against the crowd	You won't be easily swayed by the cautious counsel of others
You won't win a lot or lose a lot	You won't see problems where others might
If something goes wrong once, you won't give it a second chance	You won't have the regrets that accompany lost opportunities
	You won't have a predictable life pattern

- ❖ 'I'm in for the thrill of the chase.'
- ❖ 'Variety is the spice of life.'

Lucky people believe in themselves: they know they can do it and they can sort it out if it goes wrong. If it doesn't work out, they pick themselves up and try again. For them, setbacks are learning opportunities. They don't worry what other people think and brush off criticism with a laugh. It does not occur to them that failure is an option. In fact, they don't see themselves as risk-takers, but think it's a natural way to behave. One person's risk is another person's logical decision.

So where do you fit?

Rate the following on the scale of one to ten, where one is low risk and ten is dicing with death!

- ❖ committing to a bungee jump;
- ❖ investing £5000 on a red-hot share tip from a friend;
- ❖ betting £10 on the favourite in the 3.30 at Kempton Park;
- ❖ selling up everything to pursue your life's dream;
- ❖ walking along a dark country lane at night;
- ❖ accepting a new job when you are well-rewarded and happy where you are;
- ❖ confiding a deep secret to a friend;
- ❖ putting your house on the line to secure an overdraft for your business;
- ❖ going to a party where you know no-one;
- ❖ ignoring the advice of trusted friends; and
- ❖ buying a house in France or Spain.

There are no right or wrong answers – risk is relative. See where you stand and try a new approach to risk.

Why would you want to? Because experimenting works! It opens new horizons and creates new mental pathways. You look at things with fresh eyes, think differently and gain new perspectives.

Taking risks helps you forge new pathways through the jungle of life

Imagine you live alone in the jungle and you have hacked a pathway from your camp to the riverside. This route is a good one; it is familiar, all hazards have been removed and over time, it has become well-trodden and smooth. It holds no surprises and takes you where you want to be. You are lonely and life is rough, but you survive.

Unknown to you, in another part of the jungle there is a clearing with log cabins, electricity, clean running water, a first aid post and a group of stimulating people.

Unless you were to experiment with new paths to the riverside, you would never find the clearing and new way of life. Hacking new routes through the jungle would bring the heady mixture of disappointment, surprises, dangers, rewards and exposure to new and different things.

The reward for the risks you take will be more than worth it. You will gain confidence, a more open mind and increased possibilities and choices. Well, you say, what sort of things do I have to do to increase my Risk-Ability? Here are some suggestions you can experiment with immediately, so pick up your machete and hack away.

Brilliant Ideas for using Risk-Ability to increase your luck

Your luck will change if you allow new ways of thinking

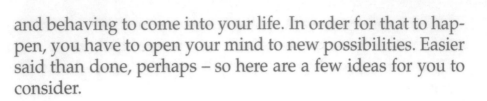

and behaving to come into your life. In order for that to happen, you have to open your mind to new possibilities. Easier said than done, perhaps – so here are a few ideas for you to consider.

Say 'yes'

First of all, experiment by saying 'yes' when normally you would say 'no'. Remember that studies show that it takes six weeks to form a new habit, so don't think that if you do it once you have altered your life! When you do things differently, you expose yourself to new situations, people, ideas and opportunities. *Do things differently – do different things!*

Daily routine

Start by asking yourself, 'What can I do differently today?' Look at your daily routine and work out what you could do to change it.

Get up at a different time

If you are a creature of habit, leaping out of bed before the alarm goes off at seven o'clock on the dot, why don't you get up half an hour earlier? Or even half an hour later – if it doesn't mean that you will end up getting sacked!

Listen to something different

While you are brushing your teeth, turn on the radio – or change the station if you do this anyway. If you never watch breakfast TV, turn it on. If you already do, turn it off.

Change or start an exercise pattern

If you are a natural sloth, get out your trainers and run

round the block. If you usually go to the gym in the morning, go for a run through the streets instead.

Change your newspaper

When you buy your daily newspaper, change it. Find a different newspaper, preferably one you think you loathe, and experience it anew. Or don't buy one – watch TV news instead.

Travel different ways

Look at how you travel to your place of work or school. Have you ever tried the bus or scrounging a lift from a neighbour? Or walking somewhere instead of jumping into the car?

Choose a different route

Do you always go the same way to your regular haunts? Pretend you are a politician and have to shake the terrorists off your trail by taking an ingenious new route every day. This way, who knows what you will see or who you will meet on your travels?

Do something different at work

What happens when you get to work? Say something different to the first person you meet. While you are at work, drink tea instead of coffee and answer your telephone in a different way. Think about it – we bet you say the same thing in the same way in the same tone every time you pick up the telephone receiver.

Move the furniture

Stun people with the radically new you. Sit back in your chair at work or at home and look at your surroundings. Why not move things around? Move the furniture, move the ornaments and make both your home and work environments dif-

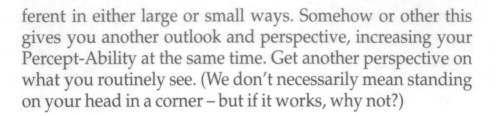

ferent in either large or small ways. Somehow or other this gives you another outlook and perspective, increasing your Percept-Ability at the same time. Get another perspective on what you routinely see. (We don't necessarily mean standing on your head in a corner – but if it works, why not?)

Have creative lunchtimes

Think about lunchtime and decide to do something different. Eat something different and choose to eat somewhere else with people you may not often see. Stretch your social boundaries and see what happens. This will also increase your Socia-Ability.

Communicate in a different way

How many times a day, a week or a month do you usually ring your friends and family? You could change it around and ring them when least expected.

Or indeed you could write a letter, or send an e-mail or a text message instead. Surprise others with your ability to do things differently and watch to see if they, in turn, will respond differently to you.

Change your answerphone message and change the tone of voice that you use to say it. When you are sending an e-mail, think if you could telephone instead.

When you are surfing the Internet, use a different search engine and seek out different websites.

Try something new

You could always try a new sport or activity. You could visit a theme park, go on the scariest ride and scare yourself witless – and then do it all again.

Think about stretching your academic or vocational learning and sign up for a course that is nothing to do with what you already know or have an affinity with. Think about your career, read the job advertisements and apply for one that may be slightly beyond you. Choose things that you have either been putting off for ages or find something you have been avoiding and just get on and do it.

Change your planning habits

Some of us like to work with lists, plans, spreadsheets and diaries, and with scrupulous habits of punctuality. If this is you, then change it. Go to the supermarket without a list and see what you end up buying. Instead of planning your holiday logically and meticulously, stick a pin in the map and plan a weekend wherever the pin lands. Turn up late and see how others react. See what it feels like to be filled with insouciance. On the other hand, if you are already like this, start making lists and shock people with your new-found punctuality and meticulous need for order and plans.

Act as if ...

No matter what you feel deep down inside, act as if you are confident, rich and successful. When wise counsel advocates caution, challenge it and do it anyway. Remember that when something goes wrong, you can always give it another go.

Learn from your regrets

Look back at opportunities you have missed and count up any regrets. Make new decisions based on this.

The new you

Look in the mirror and think what you can change. A new hairstyle, perhaps – or a new colour? A new wardrobe? A new style of make-up?

Pick the opposite

Whatever you do regularly without thinking, stop and think of the opposite. Then just do it.

- ❖ Take time to relax when you are in the greatest rush. You could stop and look at something close up, such as a flower, a pebble or a leaf.
- ❖ Try writing something with the hand you don't normally use.
- ❖ If you never look at the Stock Exchange, decide what you can afford to lose and then put a pin in the *Financial Times* Share Index and invest in that stock immediately.
- ❖ Make up your own list of opposites.

So change!

Changing your behaviour in small and large ways will expose you to opportunities that might not have come your way before.

We often settle for the safe option. You might not like your boss, you might be frustrated with the long commute into work or feel you are not developing your career in the way you had hoped, but the actions required to change might feel too risky. Why settle for less than you deserve when the solution lies in your own hands?

Brilliant Ideas pushed to the outer limits

Explore the outer limits

One of the best ways you can take a risk and expand your horizons is to go through all the *Brilliant Ideas pushed to the outer limits* sections in this book. If you're feeling daring, stick a pin on an 'outer limits' page. Commit to yourself that you will do whatever the pin lands on. Have fun!

Check your aura

Seek out an aura photographer and find out what you are radiating – or visit someone who sees auras and can give you an energy reading.

New links to people

Relationships can be the key to new opportunities. Introduce some new energy into your life by trying out a new way of dealing with the people who are or are not in your life. For example, you could try engaging with someone whose views are different to yours and aim to see their point of view without putting forward your own. If your natural style is to talk, then make sure you listen. If your natural style is to listen and defer, than put your point across forcefully. This will also increase your Socia-Ability.

Forgive your enemies!

Think of someone you have had a difference of opinion with and mentally forgive them; then go the next step and make a conciliatory approach to them. You could even find someone who you think has done you wrong and ask for their forgiveness too. Think of a recent unresolved misunderstanding and apologise unreservedly.

Imitate someone you admire

When you are thinking of where you would like to be and what you would like to become, think of someone you know who you admire, who takes risks and is successful. Ask yourself what they would do whenever you are faced with a tough decision. Find a way to spend a day with them listening and asking questions only.

Think of someone you meet regularly whom you dislike. Decide to like them, act as though you do and see what happens.

Say your piece

If you think your voice is not always heard in the debate or the argument, decide to be forceful. Be direct, say what you think and make an impact – always being careful not to get sacked! This does not mean being rude or, as they say in Yorkshire, 'calling a spade a bloody shovel'. It means working on the assumption that you have a right to be listened to if you are able to add value.

Explore the extremes

Seek the company of people who live life at the edge. Watch them closely, listen to what they have to say and work out if there are any useful tips for you.

Tell your grandchildren

What great stories are you going to tell your grandchildren? When was the last time you took a chance, grasped an opportunity or threw caution to the wind? Take the Rocking Chair Test and imagine yourself at the age of 80, looking back towards now. Will you be smiling with satisfaction at the risks that you took or wincing at the things that you let slip by?

So what's stopping you from going that extra step to take something new and different and take a risk that could transform your luck?

Luck Master 5: John Dargan

John Dargan is the Group Chief Executive of Worldmark, a global multisite manufacturer and supplier of labels to the electronics industry. When he joined the business it was a single-site subsidiary of a PLC based in Scotland; under his leadership, it has been transformed in terms of ownership, scope, values and ambitions.

He brought to the business his passion to do things with excellence and a belief that all things are possible. He knows how to lead and manage people, how to turn things on their head, and how to find a perspective that no-one knew existed. He fires people up and brings out the best in them. I wanted to know if he attributed any or all of this luck so I tried to track him down.

He was neither in Scotland nor in Mexico, but I finally found him in China as this was, he told me, where the business needed him most. Was it a problem for him to be in a remote region of China? No, not for John, as reassessing and realigning his priorities is what he does best.

John does not seem to think that luck has played a part in his success. He believes he is the hardest-working person he knows. His achievements have not come easily to him but have been fuelled by a total belief in what he is doing and a dogged determination to do what he set out to do and to do it on his terms.

As John says, 'I do what I say I am going to do' – no room there for the intervention of luck, be it good or bad. Nonetheless, life at Worldmark for John has not been a bed of roses. Hindsight demonstrated that its management buy-out had been completed at the top of the market. The company faced a constantly changing marketplace, and its customer base was reinventing itself, transferring its business to Asia to take advantage of low-cost labour and a major new opportunity.

John saw that Worldmark had to change, so he decided to mirror his customers and follow them to Asia. Getting to grips with the marketplace would be critical, so he decided that he needed to drive it by being on the spot, living in China and setting the standards for the new manufacturing facility. By doing so, he could see just what he had to do to be successful.

Revenues are forecast to double in the next three years and I wanted to know whether we could attribute them to luck or to the skills of a gifted and tenacious leader. This is the man who walks the floor of the factory in China and talks to the Chinese workforce in his own version of Mandarin. I can picture the giggles and chatter as he does so, lifting their morale and motivation to work hard for this strange creature.

One day he is in China, the next he is in Mexico, yet if you telephone him, he always seems relaxed and glad to receive my call. His energy and zest for life are second to none. He takes opportunities and chances as they occur and then works at them until they produce the right result.

John's scores on the Luck Questionnaire are always six – he is one of a small minority who endorses every single indicator whole-heartedly. He is therefore the one who accepts responsibility, takes chances where others might not, knows vast numbers of people and keeps in touch with them, and he sees things through. He has a strong reliance on his gut feel and intuition, takes a positive view of every situation, and knows himself well.

He says that he isn't lucky and insists it is down to hard work and energy. It seems to me that he behaves like a lucky person, with all of the attributes of someone who is going to make life go his way.

4

Sense-Ability

> 'Trust your hunches. They're usually based on facts
> filed away just below the conscious level.'
> – Dr Joyce Brothers

Sense-Ability is the skill of using all our senses and feelings to heighten our awareness of lucky opportunities. It includes using our emotional intelligence, gut feel and intuition. It recognises the value of coincidence.

Result? Confidence to rely on inner voice.

Sense-Ability and what it means for you

Sense-Ability is about gut feel and intuition

If we trust our gut feel, it could prevent us from falling into situations or traps that we might be tempted to describe as

---

If you want to know more about Sense-Ability, read Case Studies 1 (page 192), 4 (page 208) and 7 (page 222)

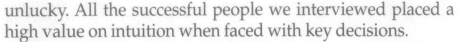

unlucky. All the successful people we interviewed placed a high value on intuition when faced with key decisions.

Sense-Ability means being aware of our environment, so that we can distinguish between the opportunities that will and won't work well for us. When Sonia Gandhi decided to turn down the post of Prime Minister of India, she said that she had made her decision by listening to her inner voice: 'I follow my inner voice. Today it tells me I must humbly decline this post.' She went on to say, 'It is my inner voice, it is my conscience.'

The importance of heightened awareness

Sense-Ability is also about awareness of our body and feelings. People with highly developed Sense-Ability have developed a gut feel or an inner voice that 'speaks' to them, giving them guidance about which path to choose when faced with choices. They pay attention to their bodies and listen to the signals they send – both emotional and physical. This resource is one of the most valuable we can develop if we want to increase our luck. Much misfortune can arise when people proceed on logic alone.

Mark Thompson, now Chairman of the BBC, had always said that he would decline the role if offered it. When asked why he changed his mind, he said 'it was what I felt at the time'. He went on to say that he felt it had a bit of a 'new age' feel to it, but believed that he had been the result of balancing between conscience, pressure and facts.

Perhaps you can think of situations in your life where you have ignored your gut feel or inner voice. You have gone ahead with a project, a relationship, a purchase or investment when you did not allow the wonderful wisdom from this resource to surface.

Our schools and university education teach us well how to make decisions based on information and logic. There are few, if any, study courses on how to improve your gut feel!

Frank is the chairman and chief executive of a company that developed the concept of superstore retailing in an unglamorous part of the marketplace. From small beginnings he now leads a multimillion-pound operation, with superstores all over the country. He views gut feel and instinct as a key part of his success.

Every business person is faced with situations that come with some degree of evidence attached to them. Frank believes that if you are a good leader, you must be able to deal with these different situations in different ways. There are some situations where it is perfectly possible to conduct a logical analysis, where you have seen similar situations before: you can see the factors involved and logically conclude that you are going to take a certain course of action. This is where business knowledge and skills count most. These can be taught and indeed *are* taught at colleges and universities. Add good business experience into this mix and, in Frank's experience, you have a powerful combination that will work in many situations.

There are other situations, however, where Frank believes that there needs to be a different way to approach things. He believes that a leader's job *really* starts when the evidence runs out – when you're faced with situations that you've never met before and where there are umpteen possibilities but nobody really knows which one is the best option. A leader's job in this case, he says, is to choose between one of two options:

The first option is to act in the absence of signposts, take a risk and get your people to follow – and the more people who follow, the better the chance of success. Thus, having the sense of *knowing* when you can move ahead in the absence of all the facts, and being able to take your team with you, is key. Frank works on the principle that even if you are slightly off-target, it is better to have everyone moving in the same direction. That way, you can agree to go for the same goals and adjust to circumstances as you go along, rather than waiting for all the facts and figures to determine the 'right' course of action. For him, gut feel is made up of intelligence, training, feeling and experience, which combine together at an unconscious level. When listened to, they will give direction in the absence of information

The second option, in Frank's view, is that occasionally, the best move is to take a decision in contradiction of the evidence. This kind of decision is to do with gut feel, confidence, being prepared to isolate yourself and being seen to take a big personal risk.

Frank's motto here is 'If you get it right, people don't actually realise when you're wrong!'

He should know. It is not luck that led to his company being featured in the *Sunday Times'* list of Britain's 100 Fastest Profit-Growth Firms 2004. It is Sense-Ability at work.

Why is intuition frequently ignored as a factor of luck or success?

The conundrum would seem to be that there are two parallel spectrums that often get confused. First of all, emotion is seen as being at the opposite side of the spectrum to logic. Secondly, gut feel or intuition is often confused with inappropriate emotion – as shown in Figure 4.1.

For example, take the work situation 'the bottom line', where facts, information, objectives, cost-benefit analyses, business cases, project plans and rational arguments are all rewarded.

These attributes are linked with an unemotional approach, since emotion is linked with rashness and foolishness

The focus of MBA programmes is to train minds in analysis information, reason, logic and data. Very few MBAs place any value on decision-making reached through gut feel or listening to an inner voice. For the MBA graduate, it is important to be able to track every element that goes into strategic analysis. Logical thought processes and trained minds matter most.

The people we interviewed agreed that all of this is very valuable, but also knew that there is an extra unqualifiable dimension to their decisions.

On their own, logic and relational analysis bring only one valuable perspective to business; if we also have excitement, enthusiasm and the thrill of the emotional involvement of the outcome, the business gains energy and pace, and a different momentum – propelling it to its goal.

Luck and balance

Luck is about balance, knowing when to place your confidence and reliance on facts, and when to fly in the face of the data and go with the gut feel. Just as 100% reliance on logic and information is not enough, neither is it sensible to

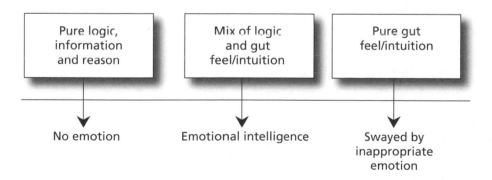

Figure 4.1 *Emotion versus logic*

make critical decisions based just on how you feel. Perhaps the answer is to pay attention to your instinct but reserve final judgement until you know the facts – and *vice versa*.

Some questions to ask yourself

When you meet someone socially, how often do you make an instant decision about whether or not you like them? How often are you wrong?

What happens when you meet someone and the hackles rise on the back of your neck? Equally, what's going on when you meet someone and instantly feel that you have known them all your life? You may have no logical explanation for your reaction and you will have no evidence to support it. Do you listen? *Should* you listen? This is where balancing instinct and evidence comes into its own. True Sense-Ability will play its part in enabling you to come to the right conclusion.

Create your own success: create Sense-Ability

What will happen if you don't have Sense-Ability?

A lack of Sense-Ability in the aspiring lucky person will mean that their decisions could be two-dimensional. Things will be judged to be right or wrong, or black or white, without recognising that there is sometimes a need to embrace opposites.

By filtering out the potential relevance of information that seeps into the conscious mind from an unidentified source, there is a danger of overlooking lessons from the past that have been consciously forgotten but unconsciously remembered.

If you don't have Sense-Ability, you may think there is one best way. You will miss the value of paradox, contradiction and coincidence.

What won't happen if you don't have Sense-Ability?

If you don't listen to that inner voice that comes from Sense-Ability, you won't be able to see beyond the surface.

You won't have the breadth of vision or thought that takes you into the next dimension.

You won't spot the next step that takes you into the quantum leap of luck. You may see what is obvious but you won't be able to read between the lines.

What won't happen if you do have Sense-Ability?

The Sense-Ability approach to life means that you don't get bogged down in mere detail. You won't miss the clues and signals, and you won't be frightened to trust your judgement when others are questioning you.

You won't jump in feet first without testing things out using both logic and intuition. You will look after your health because you won't disregard the signals from your body.

What will happen if you do have Sense-Ability?

If you have the benefit of Sense-Ability, you will have an intuitive ability to maintain equilibrium in relationships, a work/home balance, what you give to others and what you give to yourself. You will get the balance right in what you ask for and what you receive.

It will be as though you have a mental set of automatic scales that ensure nothing gets out of kilter. If you live by the premise that what you put in is what you get back, a well developed Sense-Ability will unconsciously maintain the flow.

You will be able to factor in the unexpected connection and intuitive possibilities that other people don't see. Your luck will be enhanced by an indefinable X-factor that is beyond logic: something you can't physically see, hear or touch.

You will be seen by others to have the magical touch, giving the inspirational leadership of the lucky entrepreneur.

Make life go your way

The effects of having or not having Sense-Ability are shown in Table 4.1.

Brilliant Ideas for using Sense-Ability to increase your luck

Go through these brilliant ideas and use your gut feel to help you to decide which ones will work best for you, drawing out something else within you that will enhance your lucky skills and make life go your way. *We* know that all these Brilliant Ideas work brilliantly. But don't take our word for it – try them out, see how you feel and then choose for yourself. Remember your need to stretch your Sense-Ability, so when we invite you to go to the outer limits, suspend your disbelief and just try it out. Have fun!

Open your communication channels

Hannah worked at an international airport on the information desk. Above the desk was a huge sign, 20 feet long by 6 feet high, saying 'Information Desk'. There was another large sign on the desk itself. She observed that many anxious passengers would walk within a few feet of the desk and stop fellow passengers or other airline staff to ask where the information desk was. They just couldn't see it because their channels of communication were blocked by stress.

98

Table 4.1   *Make life go your way*

What will happen if you do have Sense-Ability?	What will happen if you don't have Sense-Ability?
You will be tuned in to possibilities	You will only see what's there
You will see beyond the facts	You will be driven by facts
You will make good use of all your senses, including the 'sixth sense'	You will base what you do solely on past experience
You will make intuitive leaps	You will work things through on a step-by-step basis
You will be an inspirational thinker	You will assume that there is only one obvious way to do things
You will pay attention to your inner voice when you make decisions	You will use only logic to solve problems
You will ask yourself the meaning of coincidences in your life	You will have narrow horizons
You will have a feeling of equilibrium in your life	You might take the wrong job

What won't happen if you don't have Sense-Ability?	What won't happen if you do have Sense-Ability?
You won't get the higher margin or value gained through making connections	You won't be complacent
You won't spot coincidences – and if you do, you won't see the significance	You won't miss the underlying meaning
You won't have a balanced view	You won't get stuck in detail
You won't connect well with your environment	You won't be a slave to the facts
You won't use what your unconscious mind is flashing up	You won't be subject to wild mood swings
You won't have a wide perspective	You won't sacrifice long-term advantage for short-term gain
	You won't jump at the first option
	You won't feel that your life is out of balance

When we are stressed, we don't take in information as readily as we do when we are relaxed. Nor can we express ourselves as well; somehow our channels of communication become blocked. Bringing ourselves to the present and noticing what surrounds us takes us away from the stresses of everyday living and allows us to appreciate that we are part of a larger order of being. If we connect with our environment, the channels of communication begin to free up and we are more resourceful.

The time of day

Here's an experiment you can try. If you have a (non-digital) watch, take it off your wrist or make sure it's covered up.

Now draw your watch face. When you have finished, compare it to the original. How accurate were you?

Most people find that their drawings are not very accurate – especially if the watch is not digital. They put numbers in where there are none, or miss off the second hand or the date box.

How can this be? Most people check their watches several times a day! The truth is we can look at something regularly but not see it in full. With a watch, we are looking at it to get the time, not to notice the design. Of course, when someone buys a watch, that's when the design is important. So awareness of what surrounds us depends largely on our purpose or need when we are observing it.

Those people who are more aware at every level, even this superficial one of the details of what surrounds them, find they tend to spot lucky opportunities where others might not. By developing this higher level of awareness, you will also be increasing your Percept-Ability.

Time out

There's an even more effective exercise that is particularly useful when you have a problem to solve or a decision to make.

This time you need to find an hour when you won't be disturbed. Make sure your mobile is switched off and that any other phone won't ring. Turn off the radio, TV and hi-fi. Resist having a cigarette, coffee or tea, or indeed any drink or refreshment.

Now just sit. Keep your mind clear. Aim to think of nothing – in other words, do not bring your problem or decision into the space that you have created. If you do begin to think about anything, imagine your thoughts like clouds and watch them drift away, leaving your mind clear.

What you *can* do is change your position in the room you are in – stand, sit, change seats, look out of the window, and so on. Notice how you feel as the hour ticks by – but make no judgements.

Most busy people find this exercise hugely difficult, especially for the first half-hour. It's important to persevere – after all, if your problem is large or your decision has far-reaching consequences, then an hour of your time now may save you days, weeks or even years of regret or disappointment in the future.

After half an hour or so, most people find that something wonderful happens. Suddenly they are in touch with a part of themselves that they didn't know existed. Some inner wisdom rises to the surface. At the end of the hour they end up calmer, more refreshed and clear about the next step.

Listen to your body

Learn to listen to your body. Learn to listen to your gut feel. *Luck from the past creates luck in the future.*

Think of a time when you felt really good about something that happened and thought you were really lucky. Be there now. See what you saw, hear what you heard and feel what you felt.

As you recapture the feelings, just notice where they are in your body. Everyone is different: for some people, it is a feeling of light and warmth in their chest or stomach; for others, it is an overall glow. Whatever you feel will be right for you. The important thing is to raise your awareness of exactly where that feeling is and be able to describe it to yourself.

You now know where to check in your body to determine whether something is good for you. It will be more difficult to ignore.

Now think of a time when you felt bad about something you did or a decision you made. Go back briefly and recapture the moment. Don't spend too long there – just long enough to register the feeling again and to raise it in your awareness. Again, everyone is different. For some, it is a feeling of heaviness in the stomach. For others, it's a frozen kind of feeling in their hands and arms or legs. Again, whatever or wherever it is for you is all right. This is your warning signal and can be one of your best friends. When you feel it, you will know more readily that you are likely to be choosing the wrong option.

(By the way, once you have come away from the bad feeling, remember to recapture a good memory and some more good feelings so that you don't carry the negative feelings with you.)

Now that you have increased your awareness through your senses (that is, your Sense-Ability), you will be in a much better position to make good decisions and avoid bad ones – and therefore increase your luck. You will be less likely to reject your gut feel when you are faced with a difficult choice. Your inner voice will begin to tell you what's best. So don't be surprised if people begin to say to you, 'Well, it was lucky you made that choice and not the other one'. You will know that it wasn't actually luck at all.

Luck and health

Another way in which you can get in touch with your body is by listening to the messages it sends you. Much supposed ill luck is caused through actions or decisions that are taken when people are tired or unwell. Illnesses themselves are often the result of ignoring the signals that our bodies send us.

This can, of course, be taken to an extreme, where a headache is exaggerated as potential meningitis, or breathlessness becomes a heart condition. However, many people simply abuse their bodies – sorry, there's simply no kinder way of putting it! They continually lack energy and don't check out their aches and pains early enough because they are too busy to go to the doctors.

Here's an exercise you can try. Draw a picture of yourself – like a gingerbread person. Starting at the head and moving downwards, examine yourself mentally and write down any regular complaints you get in each part of your body.

You might be surprised at how many you decide to ignore! The point here is not to get you to focus on what's wrong with you, although this exercise does highlight one of the many paradoxes that we need to come to grips with if we are to make our lives luckier. The paradox goes something like this: *Listen to your body and take account of the messages it sends. Believe that you are healthy and that you have nothing wrong with you.*

More and more research suggests that there is a definite connection between our emotions and our health. So perhaps another aspect of being lucky in health is to deal with potentially destructive emotions such as bitterness, resentment, guilt and anger.

One theory is that emotions are located in the body and that they build up over time if they are not dealt with – as such, anger is now connected with heart disease. This of course does not mean to say that every person who suffers from heart disease is angry or that anyone who had deep unresolved anger inside will get heart disease. It simply means that someone with deep-rooted anger may well be more vulnerable to heart disease than someone who manages their emotion constructively and does not allow it to build up. It's as if for some people the anger/guilt/bitterness emotions act as a corrosive substance that eats away at the immune system.

This has a certain face value. We can all appreciate that harbouring negative emotions gets in the way and cannot be good for us – most people would accept this. What they don't all accept, unless they have high Control-Ability, is that they can actually do something about it. Our challenge to you is: where do you stand?

Take a chance

The next time you meet someone and your instinct is to dismiss them and to move on, prolong the conversation, seek out the common ground and find reasons why you might like them. Decide that although they may be very different and perhaps it is not easy to establish rapport, see what happens when you work at it and see what you might learn from those who might be very different.

Emotional honesty

Have you ever been in a situation where you didn't say what you felt – when you find yourself avoiding the truth of a situation? You know what you really feel and you know that the right thing to do is to face up to the situation, say what you feel and find a way to resolve it. But you choose not to: possibly through fear, a desire to not hurt other people's feelings, not wanting to be thought badly of or being unable to choose the right words to express what you mean.

What happens is that the emotions are bottled up and because the issue remains unresolved, it drains our energy.

To change this pattern, start with something small. For example, if someone asks you if you think it is a good idea, try saying no if that is what you feel. Don't be like the people who were not brave enough to tell the Emperor he had no clothes on; be like the honest little boy.

Brilliant Ideas pushed to the outer limits

The country walk

Take a walk in the country – or just in a park or street where there are gardens. Go by yourself and speak to no-one. Just observe whatever you pass in great detail. Stop and look at the flowers, insects, grass and trees in minute detail. Feel the texture of a leaf or the bark of a tree. Examine the petals of a flower. Listen to birdsong. Notice things you would normally pass by in the normal rush of the day. This exercise has a number of benefits:

❖ It opens up your senses to what's around you. There are many lessons to be learned from nature: if you were educated in Scotland, no doubt you will have learned of the story of King Robert the Bruce who was defeated at the battle of Bannockburn and who ran into the hills to hide. In a cave, he sat watching as a spider tried to spin its web from one side of the cave to another. Six times it tried and failed – and the seventh time, it succeeded. Robert the Bruce was inspired! 'If a spider can do that,' he thought, 'then I can go back and lead my people and take them to victory.' King Robert learned the value of Stick-Ability from a spider – and the rest, as they say, is history!

❖ By opening up your senses, you will be more aware of your surroundings in general and therefore more likely to see, hear or feel things that will help you to reach your goals.

❖ It is a brilliant stress-reliever. When we are under stress, our focus goes inwards instead of outwards. By focusing outwards it is possible to take a more objective view of events, reduce the negative emotion and gain a better perspective.

The listening jam jar

Find a time when you won't be disturbed for about five minutes or so – preferably where you can hear some sounds of nature. Place your feet hip-width apart and stand tall but relaxed. Now just listen. Keep saying to yourself, 'I am listening'.

If you can do this for a few minutes, it helps to still the mind. It's like a jam jar filled with sand and water. When you shake the jar, it becomes cloudy; when you stand the jam jar still, the sand sinks to the bottom and the water becomes clear.

Our minds are like this: choked and clouded, with so much to think about and do. No wonder we sometimes can't think straight – we don't give ourselves time out to be still and to allow our minds to settle. We wonder why things don't always go our way and why we are unlucky at times, but sometimes it's simply because we haven't thought things through clearly. It can be easier to blame misfortune or bad luck instead of thinking how we might have helped to prevent a particular situation from arising.

Biting your tongue

How often do you bite your tongue and not say what you really think? The next time you catch yourself choosing your words or dodging the issue, consider the potential impact of being totally candid. Emotional honesty drains your energy, so re-energise yourself and free yourself up with the truth.

What you project is what you get

You can increase your luck by being clear about what you want and projecting it outwards. We all know this works in a negative way: just think of some of the times you have been fearful about something and, hey presto, your worst fears have been realised. You may have been bullied (either mentally or physically), or taken advantage of in some way.

The good news is that the same process can work for good things as well. Somehow or other, we send out signals in a thousand ways without realising it. These attract a response whether for good or ill. So let's use this to our advantage. There are too many stories of coincidences happening to ignore the potential advantages of projection.

Stephen is a management consultant. He is self-employed and experiences the fluctuations in business that are typical of this type of work. At one particularly worrying period, Stephen spent extra time on normal marketing activities. He also projected outwards the thought 'I need some work in January'. Within a day of doing this, his diary for January was half-full. The work did not come from any of his marketing activities: it came from a completely separate and surprising source. Coincidence? Not in Stephen's book – it had happened too many times before.

So what is stopping you from increasing your intuition and increasing your luck?

Luck Master 6: Bill Grimsey

Bill Grimsey is the Chief Executive Officer of the Big Food Group (BFG), the major British specialist in frozen foods formerly known as Iceland that also operates as Woodward Foodservice and Booker Cash & Carry.

Stealing time out of his diary required more than a lucky mindset. I used all my powers of persuasion, tenacity and persistence in order to come face-to-face this impressive leader, dressed in his Booker polo shirt and casual trousers. He welcomed me with warmth and informality as though he had nothing more he wanted to do than to talk to me about luck. Ever eagle-eyed, I spotted his suit hanging in a corner, ready for when he assumed the part of CEO for the City.

Bill has thought a lot about luck and first of all needed to define success: for him, it means being the best at whatever you are good at. He drives this through his business, wanting to support his people in achieving their own success. He will facilitate the personal development and growth of his staff, but only if they choose it. Motivation and drive come from within, according to Bill, and he should know. I was intrigued to learn more about the path he had followed to become the leader of a household name; the golden boy who had transformed the fortunes of Wickes and realised the value for shareholders.

Bill gets passionate about things that he understands intuitively. He has always gone with his intuition, knowing that he can add on practical, data-driven knowledge to back up his needs and decisions. He is certain about the need to make choices: he chose to be a generalist, knowing with total clarity when he was a butcher's boy in a supermarket at the age of 15, that he was going to be a general manager and run the whole show. He made his choice and then navigated his way towards it.

If you are going to work with Bill, be ready to work. He wants to win and throws himself at it with drive, energy and commitment. Don't get involved – get committed. As he said to me, the chicken and the pig went for their breakfast of eggs and bacon: the chicken was only involved but the pig was truly committed.

BFG adopted Breast Cancer Research as its charity last year. Bill led a team in the London Marathon as part of the fundraising activities; in order to do that he had to run 30 miles every weekend. That's what I call commitment.

Bill is conscious of the passing of time and is a whole-hearted advocate of the principle that life is not a rehearsal. Has this made him more likely to take risks? He has taken some bold steps in career terms, leaving Tesco at the age of 36 and moving to Hong Kong with his wife and children in order to run the Park 'N Shop supermarket group. His wife had to leave her fast-track legal career, the boys had to readjust to new schools and friends, and Bill had to accept that Tesco never

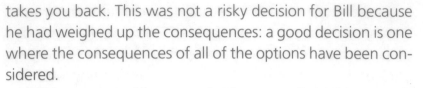

takes you back. This was not a risky decision for Bill because he had weighed up the consequences: a good decision is one where the consequences of all of the options have been considered.

Bill has strong views on mistakes as well. Making one is not such a big issue for him: it is recognising a mistake and then dealing with it that is mission-critical. There's no room for patching up and smoothing over for Bill – only radical surgery and total candour.

I still needed to know the secret of achieving business success. Bill was happy to supply it: engender spirit. Bill is strong on sports analogies and he spoke of the Saturday morning football team that goes out with low spirits, knowing they are going to be beaten. They dress like a rabble and get trounced every week. Inject them with belief, vision and inspiration and their game will be transformed. This will only happen if:

❖ they have a strategy and a game plan that can be articulated at a simple level;
❖ everyone understands where they are going and how they are going to get there; and
❖ there are some star performers to work with the utility players – everyone needs a David Beckham.

I noted that so far, Bill had not ascribed any of his success to luck. He just doesn't believe in it. He thinks you need tenacity, grit and determination, and that you need to be able to pick yourself up when you have fallen on your face – you can't just walk away. He thinks you need to have mentors, as he had in Ian McLaurin, and the brilliance of a strong working relationship, as he does with Bill Hoskins, his Finance Director.

A driven person like Bill doesn't need luck. He needs to keep going towards his goal, bringing his people with him and staving off a fear of failure. When will he know that he's been truly successful? Perhaps when he has time to take one of those motorbikes out of the garage and go for a drive – just for the hell of it!

5

Socia-Ability

> 'Getting people to like you is simply the other side of liking other people.' – Norman Vincent Peale

Socia-Ability is the talent to relate easily to other people in a wide variety of contexts. It includes being comfortable with striking up conversations with people we don't know, being proactive about keeping up with the people we do know and generally going out of our way to network.

Result? More lucky coincidences.

Socia-Ability and what it means for you

Luck is about being in the right place at the right time. It therefore follows that if you can manoeuvre yourself into a greater number of places, then your chances of striking lucky are increased.

If you want to know more about Socia-Ability, read Case Studies 1 (page 192), 2 (page 199), 4 (page 208), 5 (page 213), 6 (page 218) and 7 (page 222)

The 'six degrees of separation' theory

Subscribers to the six degrees of separation would have it that we are only six people away from anyone we want to talk to. Networking is the current vogue theme. We all know we should be doing it so why is it that some people have a natural skill for it that others don't?

What is networking?

It is a conscious attempt to increase the number of people you meet and get to know. It can be used for both business and social purposes. With a bit of luck, therefore, you can increase your luck and have some fun along the way!

Does networking work?

How can you ensure that when you network it will be a worthwhile investment of your time? How can you know that you are putting yourself in the right place? Networking can be an enormous waste of time or it can be wonderfully productive. We will suggest several ways in which you can make great returns on your networking investment.

Business networking

Business networking is about building relationships with people for a specific purpose Personal connections can add ideas, customers, products, markets and innovation, ending up on the bottom line and all contributing to the ultimate goal of success.

Meredith Belbin calls natural networkers 'resource investigators': people who like to develop contacts, explore opportunities and know how to respond to a challenge. When applied to both personal and business life, suddenly appropriate networking can broaden horizons and add new, exciting dimensions to life.

How can Socia-Ability increase your luck in business? Look at the following statements and ask yourself how many apply to you:

- ❖ I would like to be recognised and acknowledged;
- ❖ I would like to be able to find creative solutions;
- ❖ I would like to have my hat in the ring for career advancement;
- ❖ I would like to be visible;
- ❖ I would like to be at the cutting edge;
- ❖ I would like to be a decision-maker rather than an implementer;
- ❖ I would like to be at the forefront of new developments and thinking;
- ❖ I would like to expand my horizons and have a few intellectual challenges;
- ❖ I would like to have wider perspectives;
- ❖ I would like to oil the wheels of communication;
- ❖ I would like to have good relationships with the people I work with; and
- ❖ I would like to have a database of people I can call on.

If you answered 'yes' to three or more of these, then networking will be worthwhile for you.

Research shows that networking is a legitimate and essential business skill as opposed to being something that is just nice to do. It can be planned for in the same way as other business activities.

Social networking

Social networking has a different purpose. It is about extending your circle of friends and seems to be easier at certain stages of your life than others. Speed dating is the current craze, giving people the chance to meet others in a safe, fun way. Dating agencies help out people who have a gap in their lives for someone else. Fortune favours the brave – those who are prepared to risk rejection also stand to win new connections.

Networking through life

The opportunities to network are there throughout life, although we might not call it that. When your six-year-old is off to Beavers, he does not say 'Mum, I'm off to do a spot of networking'. But it is certain that he will learn some of the social skills there that will carry him through a networking life.

If there is such a thing as luck, it is all about being able to grasp opportunities as they occur. Socia-Ability is the way in which those opportunities are created through the energy we put into expanding our networks. As the saying goes, 'it is not what you know, it's who you know'.

The more outgoing and extroverted you are, the more of a natural skill you will have for easy networking. For those of us who are introverted or shy, this skill can still be learned.

Let's have a look and get some idea of the extent of networking opportunities that are around. The scope is endless – it is only limited by the extent to which you take them up.

Table 5.1 shows the path through life and the chances that are around to meet up with new people as measured by indicator five, the Socia-Ability scale of the Luck Questionnaire. This indicates the extent of your ability to network.

Table 5.1 Life networking opportunities

Age 2–6	Age 6–12	Teenagers	Income, no kids	Married with kids	Empty nest	Retired
Tumble tots	School	School/ university/ college	Networks	Work	Work colleagues	Family
Swimming lessons	Beavers/ Scouts	Sports clubs	Professional organisations	Neighbours	Regular social/ sporting fixtures	Golf
Pre-school	Brownies/ Guides	Parties/ discos/clubs	Sports clubs	Parents/PTA	Holidays	Circle of existing friends
Playschool	Sports clubs	Cinema/ theatre	Internet	School gates	Family ties	Holidays/ weekend breaks
Parties	Sunday school	Coffee shop/ pubs	Dating agencies	School trips	Dog walking	Dog walking
Ballet lessons	Theatre clubs		Pubs/clubs/ restaurants/bars	Friends through children's activities		
	Birthday parties		Parties large and small	Dinners/parties/ barbecues		
	Sleepovers		Holidays – gender and age specific	Holidays		
	School trips		Neighbours	Dog walking		
				Babysitting circles		
				Old friends		

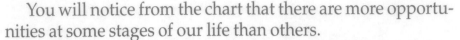

You will notice from the chart that there are more opportunities at some stages of our life than others.

As life progresses we tend to create our own groove: hopefully a fur-lined rut, but sometimes we are dissatisfied with the same old social round and boredom can creep in.

Life networking challenges

The stakes are suddenly raised when there is a dramatic event in our lives, such as redundancy, divorce, bereavement, relocation or illness. Suddenly our networks may well become inadequate and we need to think again about how we spend our time and who we spend it with. We might need our network to help us to find a new job, companionship, solve a problem, settle into a new network or find a new partner. On the other hand, we may just need to inject some interest, energy or novelty into our normal routine, as we may just be bored.

How do we change the way we live? How do we get invited to different events and become able to form links with different kinds of people?

Pay it forward

Networking is not about what you can get; it's much more about what you can give. Giving without thought of the payback – known as paying it forward – tends to produce many more dividends than simply returning a favour. Returning a favour, however, should not be neglected. No-one likes the parasite who is there for what they can grab. What you get out of networking is likely to be equal in value to the contribution you make. Achieve a sound balance in your networking and everyone wins.

One good tip for successful networking is to be clear about what you can offer when you go to any event. Consider what happens when the scales are uneven: whether we know it or not, we tend to keep a mental note of people who have not 'paid their networking round'. You can't keep on expecting other people to buy the drinks: you've got to put your hand in your pocket or you won't be invited back. You have a contribution to make, so don't be the parasite, the scrounger, the drain on other people's resources.

> Twenty-one-year-old James applied to a local prestigious gym, part of a network of leisure clubs, for a temporary job. The form was complicated, requiring photographs, referees and tailored biographical detail. He was desperate for work and thought he was well-suited to the role. The weeks went by and he did not even get an acknowledgement of his application.
>
> Six months later, when he had secured a good job in sales, he could now afford to join a gym. The local gym that had ignored his application was now ignored by him. He has already told anyone who will listen about his poor treatment at their hands.
>
> James is not unusual. We all do this and some people take it further than others – so take note!

> Alan Johnson, a senior executive with hugely influential networks, had been made redundant and was actively job-seeking. He was a prolific letter writer, e-mail sender and telephone caller, tapping into every resource of his network. He eventually found a chief executive's role in a multinational business. He joined it with a new resource – a database of all the individuals and businesses who had failed to respond to his approach. We hope you're not on it!

119

Informal networks

When we talk about networks, we don't just mean the formal structures that have been set up for business groups or special interest groups. Yes, it does include the Institute of Directors' events calendar as well as the local gardening club, but it also embraces any situation where you meet someone and exchange information. If we talk to the same people day in, day out, we will find it hard to expand our thinking and our lives. Break out and a whole new world awaits you.

Create your own success: create Socia-Ability

What will happen if you don't have Socia-Ability?

If you lack the skill associated with Socia-Ability, you will restrict your access to luck and you will never know what you have missed. You will have fewer people to call upon in times of difficulty and ill health, and you won't realise that someone else could have added value.

You will probably at some point feel isolated and lonely, spending time on your own when you might have preferred not to. You will be puzzled when you see good things happening to other people and not to you. You will see opportunities passing you by and not understand why. You are less likely to benefit from chance encounters and you won't experience the piece of luck that drops out of the blue.

What won't happen if you don't have Socia-Ability?

If you go through a personal trauma of some kind, whether it's divorce, bereavement, family illness, financial problems or family difficulties, you will often find specialist support groups to help you in ways you could never have imagined.

If you don't have Socia-Ability, it is doubtful that you will look for this help or find it in existing networks. You are likely to be sending out signals to others that you won't welcome their approach. While this may be what you want, it will detract from your ability to increase your luck.

Employees won't tell you about their mistakes, friends won't be candid with you, and if you are a parent, your children may not confide in you. You will lose the opportunities to develop individually and to develop others.

What won't happen if you do have Socia-Ability?

You won't lose touch with people who may geographically be distant but who are important to you.

If you learn the skills of Socia-Ability, you won't feel ill at ease in all kinds of social functions – even if the skills don't come naturally to you. You will be able to overcome any social difference through your own skills. You won't be dropped off people's Christmas card list and you won't miss exciting or unusual opportunities.

You won't be stuck for another point of view or a wider perspective. You won't take a negative view of other people, because you recognise the diversity of their strengths and weaknesses. You won't rule things out without giving them a try.

What will happen if you do have Socia-Ability?

Lucky people with high levels of Socia-Ability know people from all walks of life. They are at ease in all social situations and know how to behave appropriately. They recognise

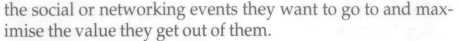

the social or networking events they want to go to and maximise the value they get out of them.

If you have Socia-Ability, you will love new social opportunities and give off the air of being interested in others. You will
be stimulated by interaction with a wide variety of people,
getting glimpses of other people's lives and then making the
social connections that come from it.

This breadth of contact may even help with the development of your gut feel or instinct, thus doubling the luck
impact by growing Sense-Ability simultaneously. Exposing
yourself to the wide world and all that's in it gives you greater
resources.

Make life go your way

The effects of having or not having Socia-Ability are shown
in Table 5.2.

Luck Master 7: Kevin Johnson

Kevin Johnson was Group Director and Managing Director of
DAKS-Simpson from 1998 until the closure of its manufacturing site in Scotland. He is a larger-than-life character who
enjoys making a contribution and making a difference to other
people.

Kindness to others is one of his guiding precepts and one
he has managed to hold on to, even in the face of making
people redundant and changing their lives. If you are kind to
people and treat them with honesty and openness, then they
will still speak to you and will retain their dignity.

He has enjoyed a successful and challenging career and I
just wanted to know if he had got there by luck or by design.
Had it just happened or did he create it?

122

Table 5.2 *Make life go your way*

What will happen if you do have Socia-Ability?	What will happen if you don't have Socia-Ability?
You will know lots of people in all walks of life	You will have a narrow circle of friends and contacts
You will gain a broader perspective on more issues	You will miss business and social opportunities
You will receive many invitations to different functions	You will restrict your potential sources of knowledge
You will meet lots of interesting people	You could end up quite isolated or lonely
When things go wrong you will have a wide choice of people to talk to and support you	You will spend more time on your own than you like
You will have a long list of contacts	Coincidences will be less likely to happen
You will always be able to explore and develop new opportunities	
You will benefit from serendipity	

What won't happen if you don't have Socia-Ability?	What won't happen if you do have Socia-Ability?
You won't always have the resources you need when you're in a fix	You won't lose touch with valued friends
You won't be exposed to the views and ideas of others	You won't be nervous about talking to strangers
People won't readily strike up conversations with you	Other people won't misinterpret your communication
You won't give anything of yourself to others	You won't miss so-called lucky coincidences
You won't tap into the collective subconscious	
What goes round won't come round to you	
You won't have difficult personal relationships	

Kevin has always wanted to maximise what he has got. He believes that there is such a thing as natural luck and he wants to make the most of it. You can't just wish for things to happen; you have to do something to make them happen.

When Kevin was an academic boffin at the age of 23, he watched his flamboyant elder brother become a multi-millionaire through entrepreneurial business success. Kevin looked at this 'Big Managing Director' brother and was de-termined to be a 'Little Managing Director'.

'Risk' is not in Kevin's vocabulary. He wants to iron out the peaks and the troughs that he believes come with high-risk taking. For him it is important to manage constantly the downside of risk: for example, if he has a baseline cost of living of £40,000, and earns £80,000, then he will save £40,000. He eschews profligacy, knowing that he needs to be cautious with the finances as money is only finite.

I wondered if this aversion to risk perhaps meant that he has missed out on achieving his potential, but no – he doesn't think so. Kevin likes being the leader and in charge, and has enjoyed this. Managing the downside of risk (or is it luck?) means that he has avoided difficult situations and minimised the impact of events beyond his control.

What Kevin does well is detail and doggedness. I sneaked a look at his tiny handwriting and formed my own view on the depths of his detail. Kevin likes to know things and to keep on learning. He watches the news, reads the papers and books, and travels and talks to people, soaking up knowledge and posting new knowledge into old areas.

He thinks of his brain as having a framework with hooks in it, and the new knowledge is hooked into the right area. Thus, when a decision has to be made, what appears to be gut instinct is, for Kevin, knowledge that has been neatly filed away for potential use.

Kevin, like John Miller, thinks that entrepreneurs keep away from detail as it holds them back: a little bit of recklessness will always help the successful entrepreneur. However, he did point out that we only hear of the ones that do well – the ones that win. We like to hear of the ones who got away with it, not the ones who lost their shirts along the way.

I asked Kevin what you did need to succeed in business if it was not luck. He instantly gave me his plan and his process, pulled from the hooks in his engineer's mind. You need leadership: someone who knows what it is about and has developed a strategy. You need structure: knowing who is doing what. You need control to gain accurate and timely information, and finally, you need discipline, so that when you get the urgent information that requires action, you act on it. If one of these four elements is missing, add it in and achieve success.

What about the individual, rather than the business process? Kevin was clear. You need a mentor and you need to network. Having a mentor is a fast track to someone else's knowledge and experience; networking can waste a lot of time but meeting the key people can make all of the difference.

Kevin also thinks that you need a good memory so that you can remember the links and names, and see the connections. Networking is not simply the social functions but the telephone calls and e-mails – staying in touch.

Kevin has a PhD in Reinforced Plastics and currently enjoys a role as a Visiting Professor at Strathclyde University. He deliberately took himself away from this academic role in order to achieve different kinds of success in life. Tenacity and detail, combined with a strong and genuine interest in people, ensured his career success. He is a forceful character with a no-nonsense style.

You know where you stand with Kevin and he knows where he stands in life – just where he wants to be. He has worked hard to stay in control of his life and in control of his luck.

Brilliant Ideas for using Socia-Ability to increase your luck

Just do it!

What could networking mean for you? We don't want you to be a busy fool or to put yourself at personal risk, but perhaps a few of the following could break the ice nicely and show you just how easy it can be if you just plunge in.

- ❖ Send one handwritten note a week to someone you haven't been in touch with for a while.
- ❖ Send one thank you card per week for every good service received.
- ❖ Keep your CV up to date.
- ❖ Arrange to meet people you talk to on the phone but have not met.
- ❖ Phone someone instead of e-mailing them.
- ❖ Have your business cards with you at social occasions.
- ❖ Read a different newspaper.
- ❖ Change the station on your radio.
- ❖ Create a family or 'social' business card.
- ❖ Create a family website.
- ❖ Send everyone a postcard when you go on holiday.
- ❖ Accept an invitation that normally you would have declined.
- ❖ Sit next to someone on the train or the bus and talk to them.

- ❖ Make a point of striking up conversations with strangers regularly, for example in the supermarket, in the bank, at the bus stop or – if you live and/or work in London – on the Tube.
- ❖ Discover what local social networking events are available and sign up for at least one.
- ❖ Organise a barbecue or drinks evening and invite neighbours that you don't know.
- ❖ Start up a network of like-minded people.
- ❖ Pay someone a compliment.
- ❖ Start a reading group.
- ❖ Join a chat room.
- ❖ Train for a marathon.
- ❖ Organise outings to the theatre, cinema or local fêtes.
- ❖ Form a team for the local pub quiz night.
- ❖ Link with a charity and play an active role.
- ❖ Become a school governor.
- ❖ Join the PTA or local residents group.
- ❖ Get involved with local children's sports training.
- ❖ Go prison visiting.
- ❖ Join the local church.
- ❖ Add your own …

Some of these are easier than others, showing that you need a few different skills to be an effective networker. Start out by working out why you are going to a networking or social event. Sometimes you may just want to go out and relax with no deeper purpose; on other occasions, you may be fulfilling a social duty, for example if it is a wedding, christening or funeral. This does not stop you from making an interesting lucky connection but it is not the prime reason for going.

Let us now focus on some more Brilliant Ideas that will help you to develop the skills that will help to make social interaction easier, more enjoyable and more productive.

What's my name?

Every person we meet says 'I am very good at remembering faces but I can never remember people's names'.

How do you remember the most important feature of anyone – their name?

First of all, make the decision that it is important to remember someone's name. We all know how we feel if someone forgets our name or gets it wrong. However we may justify our own lack of ability to remember someone's name, the truth is it comes down to one word – laziness. For most people, remembering names takes effort. There are several ways of helping to remember.

Use it or lose it

The first and most obvious way is to repeat the name immediately after someone has told you what their name is. Use it again at the first opportunity.

Label

Imagine a label with the name written on it and place it mentally above the head of the person and to the left as you are looking at them.

Character line

When you are introduced to someone, form a mental link between them and someone you know. This can be someone from history, fiction or television, someone with an unusual name – or even the name of a pet! The only criteria are that you must be able to picture this person. Picture that person's face and/or body standing beside the person you are looking at, perhaps looking over their shoulder. Take a mental snapshot so that whenever you see that person again you will recall the snap.

Picture names

Some first names, such as Dawn, Heather, Daisy, Lily or Hazel, lend themselves to pictures. Form the picture of that name and link it to them in some memorable way. For example, with Dawn, imagine her standing against a backdrop of a wonderful, colourful rising sun, or having two eyes that are sunshine yellow.

Wildly creative

Other names do not allow themselves so readily to this, so creativity and humour is needed. In this case, the more outrageous your imagination, the easier it will be to remember the name. For example:

* Anne is *âne*, French for 'donkey' – picture one with a nice straw hat and then put Anne sitting on it, smiling;
* Mark – picture a big tick in a book or place a book beside his head ('bookmark'); and
* Catherine – imagine the Catherine wheel on bonfire night, spinning around.

The more of your senses you can incorporate into this system, the more effective it will be.

Dingbats

Remember the puzzles called Dingbats?

One technique for remembering names is to use the same process. Thus when you meet someone, break the name down into a format that helps you remember. For example:

❖ Bunty = bun + tea;
❖ Carmen = car + men.

Having mastered the art of remembering everyone's name at the first time of telling, make sure that you demonstrate the skill by using it immediately.

Establish a warm link

Sometimes you forge a warm link or rapport with someone instantly and naturally. You feel that you are on the same wavelength and that you've known them for a long time. How can you make this happen when it does not occur naturally?

Body language matching

If the person you are talking to is standing up or sitting down, make sure you do. Look at their physical posture or the position of their arms and legs, and match it. Look at the angle of their spine and copy it, similarly with the tilt of their head.

Maintain good eye contact with the person without staring. Pay attention to the seating arrangements. Do you want to be on the same side of the desk or the opposite? What message are you trying to get across? For most people, sitting at a 45-degree angle is most comfortable.

Space

Manage the balance between having a yawning physical

gap between you and the other person, and being too close for comfort. Don't be a space invader.

Tone of voice matching

If you are a fast talker, have you ever felt impatient with someone who talks at half your speed? Alternatively, if you are someone who speaks slowly, do you feel you are being pushed and rushed by someone who talks nineteen to the dozen? Neither of these produces a feeling of rapport, so if it is important for you to create a relationship, it will be up to you to change the speed of your voice to match the other person's. Exactly the same principle applies to volume and pitch.

Word matching

Words are also very powerful if you want to accelerate or strengthen the relationship you have with someone. In this case you need to listen carefully to the language that they use and reflect those words back to them in your conversation. Be careful to be subtle in this so that it does not look as though you are parroting them or making fun of them.

A useful tip is to use this in written as well as spoken conversation.

Use the Internet

Have an e-chat

If you have a burning urge to widen your circle of friends and it is the middle of the night or you are stuck at a desk, remember the power of the Internet. The simplest thing to do is to send someone an e-mail for no particular reason other than the wish to have a 'chat'.

Use your cybernetwork

If you are tussling with a problem, then try whizzing it off to your cyberfriends and draw their creativity into the process. A friend who was launching a new business sent off her ideas and her product brochures to 25 people she knew – friends, family, clients – and invited their views. Within 48 hours, she had e-mails full of ideas and perspectives that she had not thought of.

Surf for fun

Surf the net with no specific purpose other than finding out something new. Go to new websites, track down old friends from school or university, and find a new recipe for dinner or a bargain weekend break. Use these resources to get yourself somewhere you did not know existed.

Find some soul-mates

Join a chat room and link up with like-minded people – or people who differ tremendously. Gaining another perspective can be inspirational and energising. Just because you invite opinions does not mean you have to accept them. It can reassure you that you are right or help you improve.

Finding what to say

Have you noticed how some people find no difficulty in finding things to say – even with people they don't know – but others find it much more difficult? They find small talk boring or impossible. Are you one of them? If you are, there's an easy solution. Instead of talking, simply *listen!*

While you are listening, do two things. Firstly, look interested in what the other person is saying even if you are not; act as if they are telling you something fascinating and useful.

Secondly, actively search for something that you have in common.

Many people who have tried this technique have been astonished at the results. All of a sudden, someone who at first appeared to be really boring becomes someone with things in common. Rapport is established and the conversation begins to flow naturally.

Another way to find things to say is to consider what you might have to offer someone else. This works because it takes the focus away from you and onto the other person.

How to make yourself memorable

Networking is about visibility. If you are not visible and people don't remember you, then the opportunities that can result from networking are limited. Some obvious ways to be visible are in the way you choose to dress, although that of course has its dangers – if you get it wrong, you could be remembered for the wrong reasons!

Visibility and being memorable is much more about making an effort to talk to a number of people at a business or social event rather than sticking with a group of people you already know. It's about attending a number of events so that you meet people more than once and can begin to establish longer-term relationships.

In business, having a memorable business card is good. Wised-up people are now adding more information on their business cards – for example, a summary of their specialist areas. Having your photograph on your card is also becoming more common and certainly helps you to be remembered.

If you're not in business, why not have a social card? We have friends who have a wacky family card called 'FLAME':

the family names are Francis, Laura, Annette, Maurice and Emily. It's fun and it works.

Following up

Good networking is also about following up any contacts made, making a note of what the conversation was about and really caring about fostering the relationship.

One good tip with business cards is to write key details on the card immediately after the networking event concerned. How many times have you looked at a pile of business cards and not been able to remember who the person was or where you met them? Worse than that, perhaps you have promised to send them something but you have not made a note of it and you've forgotten.

There are few shortcuts to good networking. It needs to be regarded as a worthwhile activity and pursued with the same enthusiasm as other goals that are important to you. As Brian Tracy put it: 'Whatever you do, whoever you meet, remember – always give without remembering and always receive without forgetting.'

Brilliant Ideas pushed to the outer limits

Improve your relationships

Be more of who you already are

This exercise will ensure that you will not be held back by any poor relationships that you may have. These poor relationships can sometimes result from expectations that are placed on you that you cannot fulfil. It could be that you do not see eye-to-eye with someone and there is tension. It could be that they have given you unhelpful labels that you have

accepted as if they were true and that have limited your potential and growth over the years.

These labels could take the form of limiting beliefs about
yourself such as being stupid, clumsy, selfish, ugly, having no
sense of humour and being poor at particular skills, such as
maths or art and so on.

Somehow or other the people concerned are tied to you in
ways you may not realise. Their labelling becomes your reality. Getting rid of these unhelpful labels does two things.

- ❖ it will improve the relationship you have with each person concerned and increase your Socia-Ability; and
- ❖ it will free you up to be more of who you really are,
increasing your Person-Ability at the same time.

The stage of life

Find a time and place where you won't be disturbed for
a few minutes. Imagine a small stage. You are going to bring
certain people up onto it. Decide in advance who these are.
(You can invite them all, just to be sure!) In any case, follow in
the order shown below:

- ❖ Parents, brothers, sisters, step-parents, stepbrothers and
stepsisters, or anyone who has been like a brother or sis-
ter to you.
- ❖ Uncles, aunts and cousins, or anyone who has acted
like an uncle or aunt to you.
- ❖ Friends both old and new; friends from when you were
a child.
- ❖ Exes – ex-boyfriends or girlfriends, or ex-partners.
- ❖ Teachers, mentors, bosses and former bosses – anyone
in a position of authority, now or in the past.

❖ Colleagues, clients and associates – anyone you have business dealings with.

❖ Anyone else not mentioned so far that your subconscious mind thinks should be there, especially anyone you feel is not supportive to you. This may include someone who is not alive or someone with whom you have unfinished business.

The first people are your parents. Imagine them walking onto the stage. You are going to ask them, 'Are you totally willing to support me in achieving my full potential and being the best I can become today?'

If the answer is 'yes', go onto the stage, thank them, give them a hug and imagine them floating away. If the answer is 'no', ask them to stay on the stage.

Do this for all the sets of people you have decided to invite onto your stage.

You may now have an empty stage. If not, picture the people who are left. (If you find it hard to picture, simply get a feeling for who is there or just listen for them.)

Now for each person in turn, go onto the stage. Imagine you are connected to them by a silver thread. Simply say to each person, 'I forgive you. I am cutting the unhelpful connection between us so that we can both be free to be the best we can be.' Cut the thread and watch them disappear.

Now enjoy your new-found freedom.

The hairs on your neck

Have you ever had the experience of feeling you were being watched and felt the hairs on your neck stand up? Somehow we know when someone is focusing on us; we even know whether their intentions are good or not depending on how comfortable or uncomfortable we feel.

This demonstrates that *energy follows thought*. We can use this principle in an ethical and powerful way if we want to increase and build relationships. First of all, prove to yourself that it works. When you are next on public transport, fix your gaze on the head or back of someone somewhere in front of you. (Remember to project positive thoughts so that the experience is a good one for the person!) If you can see their shoulders, watch for the slight lift that indicates when they breathe in and match that with your own breathing. Then breathe out with them. Test how long it is before that person shifts in their seat and eventually turns their head round. You could try this in a café, a bar or a restaurant, where you have the time to focus to make this happen.

Next try it out at a social or networking event. Target one person who you would like to make contact with. Observe their breathing, again by looking at their shoulder movements. Focus on them unobtrusively for a couple of minutes. Then go up to them and find a way to introduce yourself. You will have instant rapport!

So what's stopping you from getting out there and finding new contacts?

Luck Master 8: Glenda Stone

Glenda Stone is the entrepreneurial Chief Executive of Aurora, an international women's network that she set up only four years ago. It now has 16,000 members and is recognised as the pioneering voice of women, working for their economic advancement.

Aurora is the Roman goddess of the dawn and has been chosen as the symbol of Glenda's determination to give women a voice.

On 13 October 2003 Glenda's achievements were recognised when she was invited to Buckingham Palace to be received by the Queen as a Pioneer to the Life of the Nation. I went to meet her to find out how this success had happened and if luck had played a part in it.

When she was five in the playground of her primary school in Australia, she couldn't understand why the boys always got the swings and the girls stood around watching. She planned a playground coup and the tables turned.

This was Glenda's first encounter with gender inequality and set the pattern for her career. She wanted to challenge the accepted principle that a world run by men with grey hair is not fair. She said, 'I deserve equal rights.'

She went on to work in the Australian Outback as a teacher, watching the girls getting different treatment – something that had its roots in the academic curriculum itself. She moved to manage the system that created the policies controlling the curriculum and recognised where the power lay.

A word of advice to anyone who meets Glenda, as you inevitably will because she is out there, every night of the week, meeting people, talking to people, stretching her network – be careful. She is glamorous, articulate, resourceful and charming, with an ability to suck you into the vortex of her passions in life. Her favourite words are black and white – 'yes' and 'no' – so make sure you are clear in your focus before you talk to her.

Glenda creates energy and creates action. She is a 'Velcro for knowledge', and believes you need to get out there and meet the people – volume is everything. The more people you meet, the more likely you are to meet the one with the answer. Networking for Glenda is just like sales. You have to crank up the number of meetings and then you have to push the number and the level of conversations that you have all day.

Heaven help you, though, if you think that merely by showing up to one of Glenda's events that you have done the job. You have got to know what to ask and to make connections. She couldn't believe the small-talk banter and the time-wasting exchange of niceties that she witnessed at the first Aurora events. She wants European women to get a bit of Antipodean chutzpah: push away the fluff and get to the core. Say what you mean, ask for what you want and then reciprocate, one of the key attributes of the successful networker.

Glenda has her own definition of success, believing that success means different things for different people in its nature, its scope and its extent. She believes that success means getting what you want. This can be anything: balance in life, a baby, a husband, a wad of cash, a Porsche.

You need to know what you want and then go for it. She is adamant that luck has had nothing to do with her course in life. All she has needed is the certainty of what she wants in life and then working towards it.

She acknowledges that Aurora was very lucky to get Price-waterhouseCoopers as its sponsor, but then said that she had worked hard towards it and had pitched it as a strategic project to gain such a prestigious sponsor, and so it did not count as luck. Her premise is that the trick in business life is to work hard towards goals and then convert all of that energy into something that could be interpreted as luck.

I wondered whether Glenda took risks. She laughed. Risk is what she is about; Aurora is constantly pushing the edges.

If they host an event for 200 people, they book for 325. They use their knowledge and take a gamble.

Glenda says a common belief is that women are risk-averse. She thinks this is dangerous and inaccurate: women are just more thorough than men, doing 60% more research, paying due diligence before committing to a course of action, thus increasing their chances of success. Glenda is ready to put the business at high risk but knows she is doing it with best chance of gaining the high rewards.

When Glenda addresses her audience of businesswomen at the champagne reception in PricewaterhouseCoopers' London offices, her driving point is that 'a girl needs cash'. If you want to get that cash and the independence of choice that then comes out of it, then you have to have one A-grade priority. Women have too many priorities and their focus gets dissipated. Success is about having one clearly defined goal and delivering on it.

Glenda knows exactly where she is going in life and what she wants out of it. The twenty-first century woman should be grateful to have such a champion of their cause. The women's movement debate has gone beyond the fundamentals that were fought for in the last century; now, the stakes have been raised and women have a resolute champion in Glenda. Luck has nothing to do with where she is and her focused, high-control, risk-taking, networking path through life will ensure her place in history.

6

Percept-Ability

'What you sees is what you gets.'

Percept-Ability is all about how we look at life, events, ourselves and others. Do we have good expectations? Do we always see (or at least search for) the positive side of negative events or people? Is our attitude to life optimistic? Do we shrug off small worries and concerns? If we do, this is true Percept-Ability!

Result? Bad luck is turned into good luck.

Percept-Ability and what it means for you

'Lucky' people have high Percept-Ability; it's about how they *see* things. They have more than just a positive view of life. Percept-Ability is also what we believe about ourselves, our life and in others. It's seeing the positive side and advantages – or even just the potential advantages – of any situation.

If you want to know more about Percept-Ability, read Case Studies 1 (page 192), 3 (page 203) and 8 (page 228)

It's turning the negative to a positive in any situation. Percept-Ability is not just superficial positive thinking or naïve optimism – it's based on a series of positive beliefs.

Percept-Ability recognises that there are good times and bad times, with the occasional intervention of chance. 'Stuff' happens: accidents, illness, broken relationships, redundancy and so on. What the bad times do at the very least is help us to appreciate the good times more. Indeed, the person with high Percept-Ability will look for what there is to learn from the bad times and use that to make their life better in the future.

How full is the glass?

We've all heard of the test to check someone's view of life. Fill a litre glass with half a litre of water and ask them to describe it. Do they say that the glass is half-full or half-empty? This gives a good indication of how they look at life in general.

What can Einstein teach us?

Albert Einstein knew a lot about Percept-Ability. When asked what was the most important question a human being needed to answer, he replied: 'Is the universe a friendly place or not?' Seeing the universe as a friendly place means we are more likely to have positive expectations; we are more likely to see the good in events and people, and to believe that things will work out for the best.

If we have a clear picture of what we are looking for, such as clear goals, clear expectations and positive beliefs about ourselves and others, this gives us a different and better starting point – one that is likely to make us luckier.

Of course it's possible to be let down by others. It's possible to be disappointed that things don't turn out the way we would like every time. What Percept-Ability is about is maximising the opportunities we come across along the way. If you choose to expect the worst and to take a gloomy view of where you are, the problem is that you run the danger of creating it. Not only that, you are also ensuring that you will never get the most pleasure and thrill of life's events when they are going well.

Theresa was a successful businesswoman. She was highly respected in her field, had many friends, a loving relationship and no health or financial worries. Yet she was not happy. She was approaching 60.

Theresa saw age as a barrier – something that would restrict her. Suddenly she felt old. In the months before her 60th birthday, Theresa allowed her age to prey upon her mind. She began to stop doing the things she would normally do: she stopped looking for new business; she took less exercise and gave up her favourite activities of horse riding and tennis. She saw fewer plays at the theatre and late-night showings at the cinema, thinking she was getting too old for them.

A week before her birthday, Theresa was rushed into hospital with a suspected heart attack. She could not go back to work for three months. By that time, Theresa had convinced herself that it was time to retire, so she wound down the business. A year later she was still telling friends and ex-colleagues how unlucky she was to have had heart problems. Had it not been for this, she believed she would still be running her very successful business. As it was she was now bored, frustrated and purposeless.

So was it bad luck? Coincidence? Or did Theresa convert her negative picture of age into reality?

The self-fulfilling prophecy

What we do know is that negative pictures make negative results more likely, thus creating a self-fulfilling prophecy. It follows the pattern in Figure 6.1.

How the self-fulfilling prophecy works

Let's say I believe I am no good with figures or money. I therefore avoid checking my bank statements because I believe I'm likely to be wrong and the bank will be right. I get overdrawn one month because the bank has made a mistake (in their favour) and I am not aware of it. I am upset and say to myself something like 'I just can't manage money – I'm al-

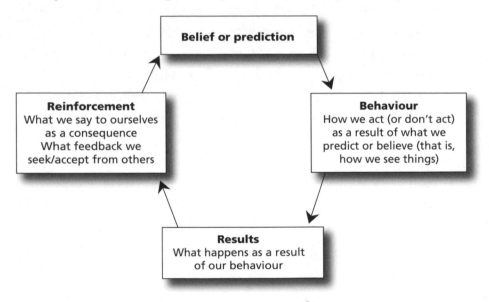

Figure 6.1   *The self-fulfilling prophecy*

144

ways going into overdraft'. This reinforces my belief that I cannot manage money and that I should leave it to the bank.

Even if I later find out that the bank is at fault, I am still not likely to change my belief about my ability to manage my finances – or my belief that the bank is always right. I am likely to rationalise the event by saying to myself something like: 'Well it's not like the bank to make a mistake like that. If I had just kept a better track of my spending, it would probably not have happened.'

The importance of holding positive mental pictures

Our mind likes to see pictures: it is drawn towards them so you can either make this work for you or against you. Our mind does not know the difference between reality and imagination. It acts upon the pictures we have as if they are true. Our mind then filters out information that does not correspond with the picture and filters in information that agrees. So you can see that a positive perception and way of looking at things can be very useful, whereas a negative way of looking at things can really hold us back.

We've probably all had the experience of not looking forward to an event, be it a visit to a relative, or looking after twenty five-year-olds at your child's party, or attending a tough meeting. All too often our actual experience tends to match the dismal picture we had in advance. Somehow it's as if we make our picture come true.

James was going on a business trip to a foreign country that had a reputation for violence. He spoke of his worries to friends. He had been told that mugging was commonplace and that no traveller was safe. He was therefore very con-

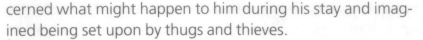

cerned what might happen to him during his stay and imagined being set upon by thugs and thieves.

When he arrived he was on the alert, suspecting every person he looked at or who looked at him. Within a week he was mugged. He lost all his money and his travel documents. In addition he was unable to relate to the people with whom he had the business dealings and so had an unsuccessful trip. Unlucky? Perhaps not. James had low Percept-Ability.

Patrick, a colleague of his from a competitor company, was visiting the same country at the same time. Patrick was not afraid. He knew that in all countries of the world it is important not to be complacent about safety but he believed that the people there were generally honest, hospitable and friendly. He looked forward to his visit, imagining all the business opportunities it would bring and how good it would be to experience another culture. This man had a wonderful stay and made many friends – as well as concluding some excellent business deals. Lucky? No! Patrick had high Percept-Ability.

Another thing to recognise is that what we believe inside shows up outside us in ways that we can only begin to imagine: *our insides are outside.*

It is true that the pictures we have in our mind's eye are somehow reflected in the signals we send out to others! It's as if what we see inside reflects somehow in how we look to others. In the above example, James went looking for trouble and he found it. He unwittingly sent out the invitation in an international 'language' and someone obliged!

Be kind

It's important to like ourselves and to speak kindly to ourselves. Research tells us that people who think and speak positively about themselves are more likely to be successful than those who beat themselves up. They say that if we treated other people the way we treat ourselves we'd have no friends left!

In the film *The Adventures of Buckaroo Banzai Across the 8th Dimension*, Buckaroo is dealing with an angry crowd that is mocking a woman. He says to the crowd, 'Hey, hey, calm down. Don't be mean. We don't have to be mean. 'Cause, remember, no matter where you go ... there you are.' Elsewhere he simply says, 'Be kind ... because wherever you go, there you are.'

Or as singer Clint Black puts it in the chorus of the song, 'Wherever You Go':

You can run from yourself but you won't get far
You can dive to the bottom of your medicine jar
But wherever you go, there you are

It is strange but true that our minds do not differentiate between what we say to ourselves and what we say to others: if I call someone else stupid, selfish or stubborn, the effect is the same as if I was calling myself those names. A good tip is to think well of others, always giving them the benefit of the doubt and searching for things to praise instead of criticise. This will lead to the sort of self-confidence that in turn will enable you to do the sort of things that lucky people do. Pathways to achieve success will open up in whatever way you define success for you.

Runs of 'bad luck'

Most people have been through times in their lives when they have what they call 'a run of bad luck'. It seems that one awful thing happens after the next and, just when they think things are at their worst, some other disaster happens. They say, 'Why me?' Worse still, they say, 'What else can happen?' and open the door to more of the same.

Sometimes one big event happens – such as contracting an illness or suffering from a disease. Take Richard, who contracted stomach cancer. He was a senior businessman who spent much of his life abroad. His condition meant that he was forced to give up his highly paid job and travel to another country for hospital care for several months, leaving behind his family and friends. Richard has high Percept-Ability. Instead of looking upon his illness as something awful he said, 'I'm lucky, you know, because it's given me the opportunity to change'.

When asked if he had ever questioned himself by asking 'Why me?', he said, 'I have – and I've also asked, "Why someone else?" '

People with a score of three or less for Percept-Ability in the Luck Questionnaire are likely to put themselves down, assume others know more than they do, presume that others are right and they are wrong, that others deserve more than they do – and so on. Whatever your score, you can increase your luck by increasing your Percept-Ability. Read on to find out how.

Luck Master 9: John Milloy

John Milloy is Human Resources Director of the Edrington Group, the Scottish manufacturer of brands of whisky such as Macallans, Cutty Sark and Famous Grouse. He is responsible for the careers and development of the 900 people employed by this multi-site manufacturing business. In 2003, the Edrington Group was included in the top 100 employers as published by the DTI and the *Sunday Times*, and John must, at that point, have remembered why he abandoned a career in accountancy and instead turned to a role that had people at its heart.

John has made some difficult choices in his career, such as when he lived in Rome and travelled round Europe while maintaining his family base in Scotland. He cheerfully dismisses it as the price he had to pay at that time in order to have a challenging job within a major US corporation and work for a great boss. I wondered if it was luck that had given him the opportunity to work for companies as diverse as Cummins Engines, the Sara Lee Corporation and the enviable role he now enjoys in a traditional Scottish brand leader. John robustly refutes that: he takes responsibility for his decisions, as well as the benefits and disadvantages that have come with them. Despite saying that, John has not had to apply for a job since 1988 because he has always been headhunted – I can vouch for that, because I tried to tempt him away some years ago. Has he always been lucky to be headhunted or is it something deeper than that? We both agreed that if you deliver results in your role and are seen to do so, recognition is a logical consequence – not an element of luck. His risk-taking was therefore based on the recognition that he would deliver what was expected of him.

At one point, John did try to say that his career could in part be put down to 'right place, right time'. However, it only took a raised quizzical eyebrow from me for him to acknowledge that he had put himself out to get where he is. When he changed careers midstream from accountancy to human resources, he went to night school twice a week for four years to gain his IPD qualification. He also commuted from Scotland to Rome to do the job he was passionate about. There's tenacity for you.

John has a strong sense of who he is and what matters to him. His whole life is underpinned by his family and their mutual dedication. He knows that the best relationships are built on chemistry, but he goes on to say that there must be integrity, values, style and behaviours for that chemistry to have meaningful substance. He does not talk about what he has achieved but reflects on the 'wonderful people who have touched my life'. I asked him if his high level of self-awareness had grown from being in human resources or whether it was something that was naturally within him. He thinks that responsibility for human resources means that you have to be able to analyse and evaluate people, and know what you are not good at; blind spots are fine, as long as they are apparent to others and are factored into the plan. I asked him what happened when things went wrong – whose fault was it then? He was very clear that responsibility lies with him. He gave me a tip, too: to gain a different outcome, break a habit and do something different. Change, therefore, is a key part of John's success: don't stand still, seek out the new and the different, and take risks.

I have always known John to be an informal, enthusiastic and engaging individual who shows real passion and excitement as he talks about what people can achieve. It is interesting that success for John is not measured in terms of material possessions. For him, it is firstly a happy and satisfied family, and then that he is seen as an approachable, open guy who is fair, decent and able to build strong teams. He has an unmistakeably steely core, with a determination to achieve the right outcome through people – although this can mean standing out against the crowd. He likes to develop the strengths and skills of individuals and teams so that a company can achieve its key performance indicators and make profits. Although financial reward is part of John's definition of success, it is not the end in itself.

Throughout his life, John has maintained a positive outlook, brushing problems and setbacks aside. He attributes this to the strong influence of his mother, who was orphaned at the age of 14 and then brought up by her older siblings. This tragedy so early in her life taught her the true meaning of problems and so she was always aware that whatever problem she faced, a lot worse could have happened. John has translated this into a mindset that means he always sees himself as fortunate, always finds a solution, maintains a cheerful and positive outlook, and is never deterred. He is very philosophical, knowing what he wants and having the confidence – fuelled by his belief that things will work out well – to make brave moves and do what is right for him.

John's character and success reminds me of the entrepreneurial Scots who throughout history have left Scotland to take their ideas and inventions into the world, and always retain what is quintessentially Scottish: clearly defined values, strong determination, a sense of humour, a clear identity and membership of a community.

Will he have a lucky future? John does not know what the future holds, but he knows it all lies within his control – that's lucky, isn't it?

Create your own success: create Percept-Ability

What will happen if you don't have Percept-Ability?

If you don't have strong Percept-Ability, you tend to see the problems, obstacles and barriers first rather than the opportunities. This could lead to opportunities passing you by

151

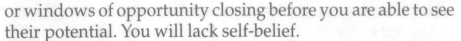

or windows of opportunity closing before you are able to see their potential. You will lack self-belief.

You will think of the worst thing that could happen rather than the best. People who have a low score in Percept-Ability tend to find that life can become overwhelming, leaving them feeling down or even depressed. They may shoot themselves in the foot or sabotage their own success because they are unconsciously determined to prove that something won't work,

What won't happen if you don't have Percept-Ability?

If this is the case, then the anticipation of problems will always outweigh the potential of success. You won't trust other people for fear of being let down. You are unlikely to fulfil your true potential because you will hold yourself back by seeing the problems.

What won't happen if you do have Percept-Ability?

Because you have high Percept-Ability, you won't hold back in the face of potential opportunities or be afraid to trust in your own abilities. You will focus on what you can do rather than what you can't and you won't look back thinking of all the things you have missed. You won't have many regrets because you have grasped the opportunities as soon as you see them.

What will happen if you do have Percept-Ability?

Because you do have high Percept-Ability, you will tend to look at yourself and generally like what you see. You will tend to have high self-esteem. You won't be arrogant or boastful, but you will tend to look at yourself in a positive light rather than a negative one – in the same way as you look at others around you. You will see yourself as equal to others, irrespective of differences in wealth, education, status and so on. You are likely to be confident in your own abilities.

Make life go your way

The effects of having or not having Percept-Ability are shown in Table 6.1.

Brilliant Ideas for using Percept-Ability to increase your luck

The language of luck

We all tend to use language at a subconscious level. We do not often have to choose our words carefully, and usually it is only in those situations that are delicate and fraught with potential problems. Why not carefully consider the language that you use and the way that you phrase your meanings? *By using language to increase your Percept-Ability you will also increase your luck.*

If things go wrong, choose your questions carefully. The sort of helpful questions you could ask yourself are as follows:

- ❖ What's good about this person/event?
- ❖ What else could this mean?
- ❖ What *could* be good about this person/event?
- ❖ How else could I/you consider this?
- ❖ What can I learn from this?
- ❖ How will this make me appreciate other things in my life?

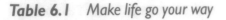

Table 6.1   *Make life go your way*

What will happen if you do have Percept-Ability?	**What will happen if you don't have Percept-Ability?**
You will always see the best in situations and people	You will see the problems rather than the opportunities
You will expect the best and usually get it	You will assume the worst
You will always see the silver lining in any cloud	It will prevent you from taking reasonable chances
You will see opportunities where others won't	Your judgment will be coloured
You will feel positive most of the time	You will be suspicious of other people's motives
Your energy levels will be high	You will worry about small things as much as big things
You will always assume that people have positive intentions towards you	You could be more prone to depression
You will get what you give	You may find yourself over-whelmed and unable to cope
You will be able to 'let go'	You may sabotage your prospects of success by focusing mainly on the downside
What won't happen if you don't have Percept-Ability?	**What won't happen if you do have Percept-Ability?**
You won't get your hopes up in case you're disappointed	You won't be beset by negative stress
You won't trust someone in case they let you down	You won't suffer from low spirits
You won't fulfil your potential, because you can only picture the problems	You won't mistrust other people
You won't anticipate success	You won't be overwhelmed by negative things
You won't have exciting things to look forward to	You won't hold yourself back
You won't encourage others to dream	

- ❖ How can I look at this so that there is a benefit?
- ❖ What could I do differently next time?
- ❖ Is there a better way to look at this?
- ❖ In what other circumstances or context could this be useful? (Remember that there is a positive place for almost any behaviour.)

When things go well, check if you are saying things to yourself like:

- ❖ Yes, that's just like me!
- ❖ I deserved that!
- ❖ Isn't it marvellous how many good things happen to me – and other people?
- ❖ I really am very fortunate.
- ❖ Expect the best and it will come.
- ❖ It's great how people can be trusted.

These are great responses.

If you are more accustomed to putting yourself down and saying 'That was a fluke' or 'I can't believe I managed to do that', then this is an excellent chance to increase your Flex-Ability at the same time as your Percept-Ability – by consciously choosing a better response to the event.

Reframing

Reframing is a way of increasing Percept-Ability. Like the analogy we used earlier, it involves getting someone to see that the glass is half-full rather than half-empty. It's rather like the army general who reassured his troops by saying, 'We're not retreating – we're just advancing in another direction!'

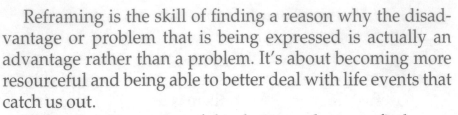

Reframing is the skill of finding a reason why the disadvantage or problem that is being expressed is actually an advantage rather than a problem. It's about becoming more resourceful and being able to better deal with life events that catch us out.

Reframing is a very useful technique when you find yourself or someone else limiting themselves, for example with phrases such as 'I'm too slow', 'I wish I could stop doing/having/being …' or 'I have a real problem with …'.

What Figure 6.2 shows is that the way we look at something affects how we feel and how we behave – and therefore what results we get. So, if we can change our perception of the problem, we can feel better about it. This affects our results and can therefore change our lives. It's that simple – and that difficult!

Here are two practical ways to change your life using reframing.

Using reframing to solve smaller problems

Reframing is the basis of much humour. So here is a fun way of using reframing to lighten up a situation or someone's view of it. You can use it on yourself as well as on others who are going through a patch of what seems like bad luck.

Jonathan: 'I walk around all the time with my shoulders hunched and looking at the ground. I feel like I have the weight of the world on my shoulders.'

Some reframes:

- ❖ That's useful – you'll always see any money that has been dropped!
- ❖ How fortunate – you'll never walk on dog dirt!
- ❖ How lucky you are – you'll never go around with your flies undone!

156

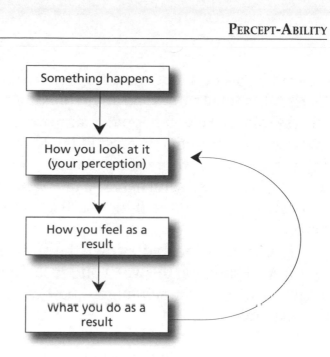

Figure 6.2 *How reframing works*

The one that made Jonathan laugh was the third one. Laughing at the problem was something he had never done before. He felt better about it and more able to cope with it.

In this particular case, Jonathan actually felt that a burden had been lifted from his shoulders and he was actually able to walk taller.

This kind of fun reframing is probably easier to do with someone else than by yourself. So if you are reframing someone else's problem, you need to be in great rapport with them – otherwise they may think you are being callous and insensitive, and do not appreciate that your purpose is to help them!

Using reframing to solve larger problems

Percept-Ability can be increased through this more rigorous approach to reframing. It is suitable for larger, more serious problems or situations. Please note that this is not a superficial, 'smiley smiley' positive thinking exercise. It doesn't necessarily make you happy; it simply helps you to achieve the frame of mind that is most likely to allow you to take effective actions and to get you the results you want. Done regularly it becomes a useful habit – a deep and fundamental way to change how you see things so that your quality of life is improved.

Here's what to do. Write down the problem, negative event or difficult situation the way you see it. Then write a list that answers, as with the reframing questions mentioned above. For example:

- ❖ What else could this mean?
- ❖ How else could I/you look at this?
- ❖ What is the benefit of ... [this situation]
- ❖ What could be good about this situation/event/problem/person – if I knew?
- ❖ In what other circumstances or context could this be useful?
- ❖ What's funny about this? What *could* be funny about this? What will be funny about this in a week/month/year/ten years?

Revisit the list and add to it. Make a note of which questions were most helpful to you. Check out how your Percept-Ability has changed for the better.

The self-fulfilling prophecy

We've already looked at the self-fulfilling prophecy. Here's how it can work in a situation when someone is applying for a job. Let's say it's the same person, the same job but two different attitudes – or perceptions. Table 6.2 shows the results.

Table 6.2   *The self-fulfilling prophecy*

How to create – or sustain – a self-fulfilling prophecy	How a self-fulfilling prophecy can work against you (negative attitude)	How a self-fulfilling prophecy can work for you (positive attitude/true Percept-Ability)
Step 1: Make a prediction or state a belief	'I'm just an unlucky person, so I'm unlikely to get that job'	'I'm a really lucky person. I have a real chance of getting that job if I put my mind to it'
Step 2: Look for evidence to support your theory	Think of all the times in the past when you have not been successful in getting a job – as well as lots of other unfortunate things that have happened to you	Think of all the times in the past when you have been successful in getting a job – as well as remembering lots of other good things that have come your way
Step 3: Disregard evidence that goes against your theory	Forget all the times you were successful in getting a job or in other circumstances	Look at the times when you were unsuccessful and examine them for things that will help you get this job

Table 6.2 (continued)

How to create – or sustain – a self-fulfilling prophecy	How a self-fulfilling prophecy can work against you (negative attitude)	How a self-fulfilling prophecy can work for you (positive attitude/true Percept-Ability)
Step 4: Go out of your way to prove that your theory or belief is true – be creative! (You may not do this consciously – it is your belief and your picture that drives your actions.)	Don't apply for the job (there's no point) Start the application form but miss the deadline Spend less time on the application form that you should – and so you won't get an interview Get an interview and go in with a defeatist attitude – so you'll be unsuccessful	Spend time and care completing your application form Find out as much as you can about the company and job Prepare for the interview: consider all the questions you could be asked and rehearse your answers Go in with a positive mindset, assuming you have an equal (or perhaps better) chance than anyone else
Step 5: Well done! You have not only created a self-fulfilling prophecy – you have also reinforced it!	See the experience as a failure or a waste of time. Feel a grim satisfaction that you were 'right' and tell everyone who encouraged you: 'I told you so – I was lucky again'	Rejoice if you get the job. If you don't, then take satisfaction from knowing that you have done your best. Look on it as useful experience for the next time

Achieving your goals

Henry Thoreau had it right when he said, 'Go confidently in the direction of your dreams! Live the life you have imagined.' What we dream about comes about 'to accomplish great things, we must not only act, but also dream; not only plan, but also believe' (Anatole France).

Let's say you have a goal. You picture it clearly in your mind. You dream about achieving it. Once you know where you want to go, you take action to reach your goal. You set off on your journey. Miraculously, it seems, opportunities suddenly begin to appear as if by magic. People look at you and comment on how lucky you are – but what you are doing is making maximum use of an aspect of Percept-Ability!

You are drawn towards the goal. You may not go in a straight line, but you are motivated to get away from what you don't want and towards what you do. You come across coincidences; you overhear a chance remark; someone just happens to have the solution or the thing you need. Are you just lucky? No! You have clearly pictured your goals. You know what you are aiming to achieve. You are using a wonderfully effective part of Percept-Ability (see Figure 6.3).

How the brain helps us

Scientists tell us that our brains are bombarded by millions of bits of information all the time. The brain can't consciously cope with all that information: it has a system for screening information. Of those millions of bits we can cope consciously with very few of them at one time. The rest are screened out.

How do we ensure that the bits that are filtered in are the right ones? *The brain chooses what is important and relevant to us now.*

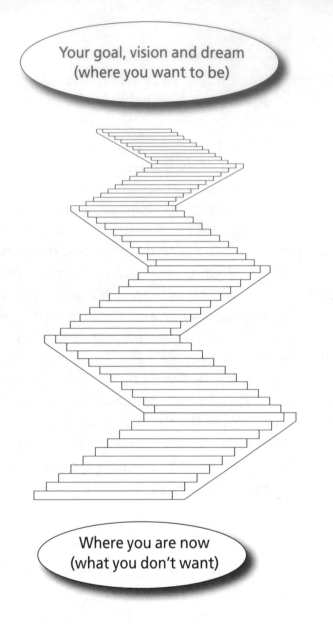

Figure 6.3 *Achieving your goals*

Link this fact to our need to achieve our goals and we can programme our brains to pick up useful information that will help us get there. A stray remark; a chance meeting; the advertisement in a newspaper we don't normally look at suddenly jumps out at us when we're not consciously looking at it and leaps into our awareness.

How many times has it happened to you that you buy something, for example a particular brand and colour of car that you believe is quite an unusual and tasteful combination, and then you spot a dozen exactly the same that you had never seen before? This is because the car has become important and relevant to you *now*, so your brain is actively seeking them – just as it had efficiently screened them out before.

Picture the day

Each morning before rising, picture the day or week ahead and what outcomes you are going to achieve during this time. Visualise all the good things that are going to happen. Imagine people – including yourself – being the best of what they can be.

List the good qualities

Choose someone you don't get on with particularly well but who it is important for you to have good a relationship with: it could be a parent, relative, in-law, colleague, tradesperson, customer, supplier or boss. List all the good qualities that that person has. Aim to see them in a new light.

Get into someone's shoes

Choose someone who seems to you to have a wonderfully positive view of the world. Put yourself in their shoes and ask yourself – how would they look at this situation? What would they do?

Real or imagined?

Prove to yourself that our mind does not know the difference between an imaginary event and a real one. Do the 'lemon test': imagine a lemon, take a sharp knife and cut it in two. See the juice drop out as you squeeze each freshly cut half. Now take a bite out of one of the halves.

Is your mouth watering? Why would that be? The lemon is only in your imagination! Our bodies act as if the pictures inside our minds are true if we see them clearly enough. This has staggering implications for our lives.

Now picture something you want to happen as clearly as you saw the lemon. Maybe it's making a speech at someone's wedding, completing a marathon, getting a job or a promotion, building a successful business or overcoming a fear. Rehearse it in your mind. Make it real, as if it has already successfully happened.

Now go out and behave normally, knowing that ways to reach your goal will come to you.

Who am I?

Draw a picture of yourself and attach some labels to the picture about who you are. As well as the more obvious ones such as 'I am a man/woman/husband/wife/manager/father/mother' and so on, think further. What were you born to be? The successful people interviewed for this book were very clear about who they were and therefore what they were good at. They said things like, 'I am a designer/retailer/trader/entrepreneur'. And remember: *whatever labels you give yourself, you are always more than that.*

Brilliant Ideas pushed to the outer limits

Magic spectacles

Imagine you have a pair of magic spectacles that you can put on in the morning – or at any time when you need to improve your ability to view things in a helpful light. So for example, if you are going through one of those times in your life when everything seems to be going wrong, put an imaginary pair of spectacles on that will allow you to see what the upside of the situation is – or to look into the future and view the time from a more distant perspective. This will increase your Percept-Ability.

'Life's Going My Way' Journal

Buy a notebook and give it a name – you could call it your *'Life's Going My Way' Journal*. At the end of every day, jot down at least one thing you are pleased about, something that has gone well or a positive experience.

Read previous entries in your *'Life's Going My Way' Journal* before going to bed so that your mind has positive things to dwell on before going to sleep

Gain a new perspective

Think of the benefits you would gain from understanding different perspectives. Call to mind an unsatisfactory situation between you and someone else.

1 Put three sheets of paper on the floor, labelled 'self', 'other' and 'observer'.

2 Stand on the 'self' sheet, facing the 'other', and recognise how you experience the situation you have chosen. Know what you would like to say to the other person. Then move away and turn around.

3 Stand on the 'other' sheet and imagine you are that person looking at the 'self'. Recognise how you, as the other person, might experience the interaction. What would you like to say to your 'self'? Then move away and turn around.

4 Step onto the 'observer' sheet and look at 'self' and 'other'. From this neutral position, notice what is happening. What is or isn't being achieved? Remember not to take sides: this is the place for objective assessment. If you notice any emotions as you stand on 'observer', check whether they belong to 'self' or 'other', and go back to that sheet. 'Observer' is a neutral position. Then move away and turn around.

5 Move back to 'self' and repeat the stages as many times as you need to gain full information and insight.

6 Decide what you will do as a result of your new understanding and realise how it will improve your luck.

The Zone

This exercise will expand the current limits of your vision, allowing you to get in touch with what you are currently unaware of. This 'black spot' exercise helps you achieve the state that athletes know as the 'zone' and educators and students know as the 'learning state'.

So if you need to be at your best at any time – whether it be for an important meeting, making a speech you feel nervous about, taking an exam, going for an interview or whatever,

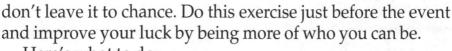

don't leave it to chance. Do this exercise just before the event and improve your luck by being more of who you can be.

Here's what to do:

1 Either sitting or standing (whichever is more appropriate), imagine a black spot in front of you that is a little bit above eye level – say on the facing wall.
2 Look at the black spot. As you stare at the spot, let your mind go loose and focus all your attention on it.
3 Notice that within a few moments, your awareness expands and you can see more of what is around you. You can also see more in your wider vision than you can in the central part of it.
4 Pay more attention to your wider vision while still being aware of the black spot.
5 Breathe deeply and continue to relax, because in this state you are opening up your ability to access information and resources that are often closed to you because of nerves or too much logical thinking.

Being in the zone like this opens the channels of communication to the creative side of the brain and helps you use your senses and intuition, and recall information easily. In this state it is impossible to feel nervous.

Imagine never having to be nervous again!

So what's stopping you from finding the easy way rather than the hard way and using your Percept-Ability to make life go your way?

Luck Master 10: Jon Trickett

'My father always said, even in the face of disastrous circumstances, that whatever happens to you, there must be a good reason – all you have to do is to look for it,' said Jon Trickett, MP for Hemsworth since 1996.

I was talking to him in his Westminster office, which was dominated by a large clock and a television screen relaying the schedule of events in the chamber of the House of Commons. He checked his pager regularly, glanced at the clock frequently and kept an eye on the events on the television screen. Life as an MP seems to mean that you have to be in the right place at the right time – a component of luck for many people, but not for Jon.

He mused over the sequence of events that brought him to Westminster and seemed to attribute success to significant opportunities that came along. He had not sought them out, but grasped them firmly when they were in front of him. Jon was elected as an MP in a by-election and had a year and a half to get to know the ropes before the large number of newly elected Labour MPs arrived at Parliament in the landslide 1997 victory. He had a friend and mentor in the chamber and he quickly established himself in the strange political environment of Westminster.

Leeds City Council must have taken a deep breath when he was elected in 1984, wondering how they could accommodate this left-wing Trotskyite rebel. This highly articulate and passionate politician, who had a clear vision for people and society, could not have been a comfortable fit in the team – but Jon was absorbed into it and was soon elected as its leader. 'How did this happen?' I asked him.

'I put my hand out and pears drop into it!' he said. Then he thought a little more. Perhaps it was not just luck for him, but an ability to seize the opportunities that have either arisen or he has created. 'Luck and difference?' he offered tentatively. He stated firmly that nothing has been imposed on him: 'everything I have done, I have chosen to do'.

Jon is firmly in charge of his life, working diligently and establishing strong personal networks. He looked baffled when asked for a definition of success. Material possessions certainly do not form part of it. He believes that the purpose of existence is the meaning that you give it. He is seeing something through that he started when he was 16. He has needed to find a voice for his values and belief systems, and is seeing through something that began when he was a teenager.

The meaning of success for Jon is to take opportunities and then work at them. It means finding the best in all situations and translating it into an action plan, and taking responsibility. He is in Westminster because of the strength of his beliefs and his knowledge that what he believes in is intrinsically right. He does not believe that he is truly successful yet. He is not motivated by money but by the need to invoke ideas that resonate. He has inner strength and determination, supported by total self-reliance.

The only meaning of luck for Jon is when events happen that are beyond your control. He was strongly associated politically with John Smith and then with Peter Mandelson, which has had an impact on his own career that was not directly of his own making. He sometimes wonders what might have happened if other people's lives had turned out differently – but not for long. Jon accepts that he is where he is through his own choices and his own decisions. Perseverance is part of his make-up and he is well-equipped for the stormy life of politics: ready for the unexpected and in for the long haul.

7

Person-Ability

'Oh wad some power the giftie gie us tae see oorsleves
as ithers see us.' – Robert Burns

Person-Ability is about knowing ourselves well enough to
recognise what works well for us and what can work against
us. This self-awareness is the skill to use those aspects of our
personality that will naturally support us in being lucky.

Result? The harnessing of all our natural luck skills.

Person-Ability and what it means for you

*Person-Ability is about balance, self awareness and
sound judgement*

Life will never go your way if on top of all those other qualities that contribute to luck, you lack the sense of who you are
and what naturally works in your favour and what naturally

If you want to know more about Person-Ability, read Case Studies 1 (page 192),
5 (page 213), 7 (page 222) and 8 (page 228)

holds you back. Welcome to the nature/nurture argument. We are all born with innate talents, interests, drives and abilities. The trick of success in life is recognising them and using them to our advantage.

Person-Ability is the Luck Indicator that supports all the others particularly well. It would be possible, for example, to have high Stick-Ability and carry on doing something that we just don't have the intelligence or flair for, and then wonder why it turns out to be a waste of time. This happened to Cheryl. She applied several times for a job that needed great strategic thinking skills. She couldn't understand why no-one would give her the job she wanted. She couldn't see that her skills were different to those that were being looked for.

The same goes for risk and intuition.

Charles viewed himself as a decisive risk-taker and set great store by his intuition – but in fact he was simply impulsive and reckless. He ignored the fact that he had previously made many mistakes on this front. He applied and accepted a new job that had good pay and an attractive bonus scheme but in a sector he was not familiar with. He relocated 200 miles with his family, resulting in new schools for the children and an unsatisfactory new job for his wife. The risk was not balanced by sufficient research or thought into what the job would really ask of him. Three months into the new job, he knew he had made a serious mistake.

The post World War II generation often found themselves under pressure from their parents to do 'a proper job' – the kind of job that would give them core wage-earning skills and ensure financial security and stability – rather than the sort of career they wanted for themselves. Years later, many of those people changed from being accountants to becoming actors or artists, or from electricians to musicians. They spent much of their lives denying who they really were or who they wanted to be and then took a chance to break out. Long live the mid-life crisis.

What this chapter will do

This chapter will help you begin to consider where your core skills, talents, passions and dreams lie, and therefore where you are most likely to find good fortune.

Just as important, it will also allow you to acknowledge potential blind spots and weaknesses. Self-knowledge is power: it enables you to maximise your strengths and therefore increase your luck.

Self-awareness governs behaviour

Businesses recognise that investment in the development of their people will bring rewards. What they really mean is that they will be playing to people's strengths, developing their weaknesses and increasing their effectiveness. The routes to this discovery can be assisted by everything from self-help books through to personal coaches, development centres, training workshops and psychometric testing. Self-awareness governs behaviours; behaviours govern results. From all of this, the message is clear: *know who you are, know what you are good at, be aware of what could trip you up and have a justified belief in yourself.*

Blind spots

Data from our Luck Questionnaire shows us that most people believe that they have high levels of self-awareness and know themselves very well. The critical question arising from this is whether or not this is true and accurate.

Take the case of David, whose goal in life was to achieve money, status and power. He narrowly missed making his millions in the late 1980s, and his entire focus for the 1990s was to build a new business. By the mid-1990s he sold his business to a PLC and was appointed to the main board – triumph! He had got what he wanted: millions in tradable shares, a main board position on a PLC and public recognition.

It all unravelled at the first board meeting. David failed to listen, imposed his views on the others and rode roughshod over the meeting. As a consequence, the rest of the board vowed to oust him and duly did so. He had taken risks, he had stuck to it when others had given up, he had grasped every possible opportunity – but he was not aware that his weak spot was his impact on other people.

Watch out for blind spots. No doubt you have driven down the motorway and been behind a lorry displaying the sign 'If you can't see my mirrors, I can't see you!'

A bus pulled out of a bus stop in Richmond. The driver checked his mirror and saw nothing coming. A second later there was a grinding of metal and the bus and a car were welded together, neither of them able to move backwards or forwards. They were stuck. As a consequence, the whole of Richmond ground to a halt and no-one could move for two hours. Someone else had to come and rescue them. The driver had forgotten about the blind spot in his mirror and had not physically checked.

How often do we check out our mental blind spots? Like the bus driver, we may get away with it ninety-nine times out of a hundred – but on the hundredth time, the consequences could be disastrous. That may be when we tell others we have had real bad luck and expect to be rescued. Who knows how many other people we inconvenience or harm in the process?

Sometimes we need someone else to point out the gaps and make us aware of our own individual blind spots. It takes courage to ask for this type of information, so if you do, decide to take at least some of what they say on board – but first, make sure it is someone whose opinions you really trust.

Our blind spots could include our impact on others, or our lack of technical skills in areas such as:

- ❖ finance;
- ❖ IT;
- ❖ organisation;
- ❖ time-keeping;
- ❖ creativity;
- ❖ listening skills;
- ❖ empathy;
- ❖ critical and strategic thinking;
- ❖ common sense;
- ❖ self-preoccupation;
- ❖ insensitivity;
- ❖ talking too much;
- ❖ personal presentation;
- ❖ judgement; and
- ❖ decision-making.

Kathleen, a very successful businesswoman, organised and ran a monthly networking club to help young people in their job search. One month she invited an eminent psychologist to address the group and share with them his knowledge, experience and skills. She sat in on the morning's presentation in order to introduce and support him. As the session progressed, she became more animated and her own contribution increased to the point that it became difficult for anyone else to have their say. At the end of the session the psychologist took her aside and said that he thought she had undone much of the value of his presentation and her efforts in pulling it all together by playing too active a role. She was upset and felt aggrieved, refusing to accept the feedback.

The 'Blackpool Rock' question

The key feature of Blackpool Rock is its identity: wherever you cut it, it says 'Blackpool Rock'. What would you find running all the way through you?
Would it be:

* I am an accountant;
* I am a trader;
* I am an intellectual;
* I am an artist;
* I am a sportsman/woman;
* I am a ballet dancer;
* I am an actor;
* I am an engineer;
* I am an artisan;
* I am a musician;
* I am a teacher;
* I am a nurse;
* I am a writer; or
* I am a farmer?

This fundamental identity comes from inherited characteristics, and childhood experiences and upbringing.

What comes most naturally to us is generally what we learnt as children. What we have been brought up to believe is the source of our motivation and drive. This can either support us or hold us back; for example, you could say that it is possible for two people to have the same experiences yet for it to affect them differently. If your parents were unemployed when you were a child, it could have either become a template for your own future or given you the drive and determination to create a different lifestyle.

Sometimes, our motivation springs from a desire to get away from what we don't want just as much as going towards what we do want.

The time when you need your self-awareness is at the big life events that are crossroads in your lives. These could be:

- the death of a parent;
- a sudden downturn in financial circumstances;
- illness;
- losing a job; or
- relocation.

Remember the equation $S + R = C$ (situation + response = consequence)?

Our response to any given situation will radically affect the consequences or results. How we *choose* our response has its roots in our upbringing and our self-knowledge. Over-estimating or underestimating our capabilities could skew our lives from a successful path to one of regret or failure. At this point, we might then attribute it to good or bad luck – resulting from our parents and social status, our education, our environment, our health, or the breadth of our learning.

177

The truth of the matter is that self-awareness allows us to choose the best option available at the time, overriding the way we may have been programmed to think of ourselves and our capabilities.

In the film *Billy Elliot*, the barrier that Billy has to overcome in his desire to be a ballet dancer is that he belongs to a family of miners in a Yorkshire pit village. He is flying in the face of convention, tradition and his family values. In his case, his passion for dancing propels him to success and allows his natural skills to flourish. Billy follows his own dream, not someone else's. He creates his own luck by recognising where his talents lie and pursues them.

Create your own success: create Person-Ability

What will happen if you don't have Person-Ability?

If you don't have Person-Ability, you could end up taking on courses, jobs or projects that you aren't capable of doing. You could irritate the people around you by being either too self-effacing or too arrogant because there is a mismatch in how you think you are coming across and how you are seen by others. You won't know why things grind to a halt or why you are not getting what you think you deserve. You will be baffled and at a loss to understand what's going on. You may have many talents and never fully develop them.

What won't happen if you don't have Person-Ability?

Life will be a frustrating puzzle. If you don't recognise who you truly are, you won't become who you are capable of becoming. You won't really know your strengths and weaknesses so you won't know which ones to take advantage of. You won't understand why people don't understand you.

You won't know how to accept compliments gracefully because you won't know what they are applauding. When life spirals out of control, you are unlikely to have sufficient resources to get back on an even keel. As the old adage goes, 'he who knows not and knows not that he knows not is a fool – shun him'.

What won't happen if you do have Person-Ability?

Good self-awareness means that you won't waste opportunities or let something good pass you by. You'll avoid making many of the life-shattering mistakes in your career or relationships that others do. You won't take on something that you are incapable of doing well. You won't make the mistake of overestimating your capabilities – neither will you underestimate them. You are unlikely to find yourself in a job where you are out of your depth. You won't be surprised by what other people think and say about you.

What will happen if you do have Person-Ability?

If you know yourself well enough, then you will recognise clearly and simply when you should be taking risks. You will make decisions about relationships using your gut feel rather than relying on the facts, deciding when to persevere and when to stop.

You will recognise that where you are today is a direct result of every decision you have ever made, proactively or by default. You will be able to distinguish between chance events and those over which you can have some influence. You will

179

have developed a range of skills that allow you to respond appropriately and flexibly to chance events.

You will see the positive side of things without being naïve. You will have a realistic appraisal of how bright you really are.

Make life go your way

The effects of having or not having Person-Ability are shown in Table 7.1.

Brilliant Ideas for using Person-Ability to increase your luck

The research data from our Luck Questionnaire indicates that most of us believe we have a very high level of self-awareness. This section, therefore, could be the one that has least application and interest to you. However, we invite you to broaden your Person-Ability horizons and explore the notion that you may not be as aware as you think you are. Act as though these Brilliant Ideas are the most intriguing element of *The Book of Luck*. As Will Schulz says in his book *Profound Simplicity*, 'I will know myself best when I overcome the fear of looking at what I truly am'.

Find a mentor

Find a person you trust to be your mentor – someone who will, through their experience and wisdom, help and guide you. Many successful people attribute their continuing success to the objective advice they gain from someone who has more experience than them and has a genuine interest in wanting to see them get on. This mentor will also let

Table 7.1   *Create your own success: create Person-Ability*

What will happen if you do have Person-Ability?	What will happen if you don't have Person-Ability?
You will have good self-knowledge	You will get in over your head
You will learn from experience and your mistakes	You will agree to do things you are not suited for
You will be able to weigh up the positives and negatives	You will be your own worst enemy
You will know when something is a step too far	You could get into a role that doesn't maximise your potential
You will know when to take a risk	You'll be hampered by your blind spots
Your judgement will be sound	
You will welcome feedback from others	You will be frustrated by your lack of personal or career development
You will have the flexibility to respond well to different situations	You will feel that others don't understand you

What won't happen if you don't have Person-Ability?	What won't happen if you do have Person-Ability?
You won't take account of your strengths and weaknesses	You won't end up as a square peg in a round hole
You won't recognise when you are out of your depth	You won't be surprised by the feedback from others
You won't understand why, when events spiral out of control, you won't be able to be yourself or become the best that you can be	You won't commit to things that are beyond your scope
	You won't kid yourself about your abilities
	You won't have to put on a front most of the time

you know when you are getting things wrong and help you to know when you should be thinking of different ways of doing things.

You could also ask friends, colleagues or family for feedback on your blind spots. You might get more than you bargained for, so grow an extra skin and keep an open mind.

In the job market ...?

When you are looking for a new job, start by writing a proper CV that really reflects what you are good at. Make sure it accurately records your achievements and your skills. Write at the top of it 'I am ...', followed by no more than 30 words that capture the essence of you.

Apply for jobs even if you are not sure about them – you may then be invited to an interview, so you can have the pleasure of a full hour talking about yourself. You can luxuriate in the pleasure of talking about who you are, what you have done, what your strengths are and what is important to you. Relish that hour, because it will be back to harsh reality when you leave the interview. Sit down and reflect on what you said and what you did. Be cruel to yourself and use that process to understand more about what and who you really are.

With luck, you might be invited to an assessment centre and then you will be hurtling down the route of self-awareness and scientifically backed 'feedback'. Use this in your journey to self-knowledge. It might be all right to fool others about what you are and what you can do, but don't hoodwink yourself in the process.

Use your downtime

When next you are bored – sitting on a bus or a train, waiting in a queue, or stuck in a traffic jam – use the time to take a long hard look at yourself. Here's what to do:

1 Write a list of as many comments as you can remember that people have made about you – even in jest.
2 Decide how valid each one may be.
3 Write down the way people described you as a child and the labels you were given. Were they true then and do they apply now? Are you acting as if they were true?
4 Write a list of things you would like people to say and think about you now.
5 How far removed from reality are they?
6 While you have your pen in your hand, find a notebook and call it your *Mirror Journal*. Note down any instances of direct or indirect feedback in it. Feel free to exclude anything that is just too beyond the pale ... you could also include in it any insights you have about your own style and behaviour.

Hear yourself

If we are aiming to find out what our impact is on others, it's important to know what we sound like.

❖ When did you last listen to your answerphone message? How do you come over – half-baked? Half-asleep? Half-dead? Have a go at putting across the style you want.
❖ Record yourself talking on the phone to friends, family or colleagues. You could amuse yourself by making sure you have the recorder handy when you get the call from a call centre when your dinner is on the table or *Coronation Street* has just started. So long as the impres-

183

sion you are giving is the one you aim to give, then that is just fine.

❖ What do you do when you are faced with poor service? Picture yourself on the fly-on-the-wall programme *Airline* and see how you would come over when your flight has been delayed for hours.

❖ Picture yourself as a participant in the programme *I'm A Celebrity – Get Me Out of Here!* How long would it be before you got voted off? Why would they want to get rid of you? Go on – be honest!

The hour of silence

When faced with a problem, sit on your own in a room where you won't be disturbed by the telephone or people. No distractions in the form of tea, coffee, cigarettes, newspapers, drinks, food or music are allowed. All you are allowed to do is change where you are sitting and change your posture, as this will give you a different perspective. Now empty your mind and aim to think of nothing. For most busy people, the first half-hour will be torture.

This will be like the snow shaker, where the snow eventually settles and the scene is revealed in total clarity – the same applies to our minds. Allowing all the business to settle gives the possibility for new ideas, creativity, awareness and solutions to arise, apparently from nowhere. We all have the solutions within us; we will access perspectives, new solutions and new openings as untapped reserves.

The fear of engaging in such a process is that we may find out things about ourselves that we don't particularly like or don't want to remember. We might come face-to-face with areas where we lack self-esteem or confidence. This knowledge in itself is a powerful weapon for change.

Alternative therapies

Open your mind to the potential of alternative therapies that will give you information about yourself. Try out:

- ❖ Reiki;
- ❖ kinesiology;
- ❖ chakra readings;
- ❖ massage (aromatherapy, marma, pressure point ...);
- ❖ hypnosis/hypnotherapy;
- ❖ herbology;
- ❖ flower remedies;
- ❖ colour therapy; or
- ❖ cupping.

And so on ...

If you don't know what these are, then you may have no idea what you are missing out on! Finding out about them will in itself tell you more about yourself and increase your Risk-Ability at the same time.

'Mirror, mirror on the wall ...'

This Brilliant Idea is about holding up a mirror to reflect who you really are.

Draw two squares to represent two picture frames. In the first frame, draw yourself as you would like to be. In the second, do you have the courage to draw yourself 'warts and all'? Can you face yourself as you really are? For most people this is not as frightening as it might appear. So take heart: *whatever you think you are, you are always more than that.*

Brilliant Ideas pushed to the outer limits

Board of directors

Appoint your own board of directors – in your mind! Choose people who are excellent at what they do. They can be people you have met and admired, or people you have read about. They can be from history or literature.

Picture them sitting round a table with you at the head. When faced with a problem or a decision, all you have to do is to ask the relevant board members for advice and listen to their replies. Remember to thank them. (Of course, it's probably best to ask the questions silently so that people don't get the wrong ideas about your sanity! The important thing here – as in many of the Brilliant Ideas in this section – is to *assume* it works and to go ahead on that basis. You will be surprised at how well this works.)

Answer the following question.

What are your top three favourite living creatures? Write them down in order of preference. Do this quickly, picking the first three that spring into mind. Then write alongside characteristics that made you choose them.

Creature	Characteristics you admire
1	
2	
3	

Here is an interpretation of the information for you to consider.

Look at answer 1 and your creature's admired characteristics – this is how you see yourself.

Look at answer 2 – this is how others see you.

Look at answer 3 – this is how you really are.

How big is the gap between the way you see yourself, the way you are seen by others and the way you really are? Are the descriptions similar or very different? This will give you some idea of the accuracy of your self-awareness.

Being centred – the coral rock

Sometimes in the busy rush of day-to-day living, we lose ourselves. We are busy trying to be all things to all people as we fulfil the various roles in our lives. We spread ourselves thinly, keep giving out and forget ourselves and who we are in the process.

Being centred is a way of giving something back to ourselves. It's about being more balanced and better able to withstand the knocks of life that can catch us broadside on.

Physical balance and mental balance are connected. This exercise helps us feel more peaceful, more grounded, more stable. To get the feeling of balance, stand upright with your feet shoulder-width apart, knees slightly bent and shoulders in line with knees and feet. Now sway gently, getting a feel for where you feel most balanced.

Imagine you are travelling on a London Tube train and you have challenged yourself to stand all the way from Heathrow to Piccadilly Circus without holding on to the overhead strap. (Have you ever done this?) Once you have your balance, it is possible to ride out all the jolts and bumps on the journey without losing your balance.

Focus on your centre of gravity, which is in your navel. Imagine all your energy is concentrated there, at your centre. This will increase your feelings of being grounded and balanced. When you get well-practised at this, these feelings are joined by a sense of peacefulness, harmony, connectedness, strength and confidence. Your mind is clear and your body relaxed in a way that feels good. You are more of who you already are.

As the Hawaiian proverb says: 'though the sea be deep and rough, the coral rock remains standing'.

So what's stopping you from being who you really are and attracting more luck into your life?

Case Studies

People in the Spotlight

Use these Case Studies to increase your luck

While researching the theme of luck for this book, we interviewed many people who are leaders in their field. By any standards, each of them is successful in many different ways.

Although the focus of these case studies is on business people who have created their own success through a demanding and entrepreneurial business career, we recognise and believe that there are many different definitions of success. Money is not necessarily part of success but is often an enabler. We could learn just as much from less high-profile people who have created a pattern of success and luck in their lives without significant wealth.

So whatever your definition of success is, you are invited to read these inspirational case studies. We know they have applications for everyone. By understanding how successful business people have influenced their luck, it is possible for us to learn from them and change ours.

Notes

❖ All the people interviewed demonstrated most, if not all, of the Luck Indicators covered in this book. Only the first interview – with Richard O'Sullivan, Managing Director of Millies Cookies – analyses and comments on all seven Luck Indicators, comparing them against his success story.

❖ In the following interviews we have been selective and chosen different people to highlight different aspects of Luck. You are invited to do your own analyses and to draw your own conclusions about the power of the Luck Indicators involved.

❖ An overview of how each Case Study connects with the Luck Indicators is shown on page 191.

❖ A summary of the seven Luck Indicators appears on page 12.

People in the Spotlight Case Studies - summary

	Control-Ability	Stick-Ability	Risk-Ability	Sense-Ability	Socia-Ability	Percept-Ability	Person-Ability
Richard O'Sullivan: Managing Director, Millies Cookies (cookie outlets)	x	x	x	x	x	x	x
Bhim Ruia: founder, the Ruia Group (household textiles supplier)			x		x		
Tom Bloxham MBE: Group Chairman, Urban Splash (property design and development)			x			x	
Peter Donnelly: founder, Eisenegger brand (sports and leisure clothing)	x			x	x		
Terry Flanagan: Chief Executive, Mason Communications (telecoms)			x		x		x
Lal Kumar: Chairman, Rajan Imports (fashion clothing distributors)			x		x		
Andy Gilbert: Group Managing Director, Go MAD (research and consultancy)	x			x	x		x
Val Gooding CBE: Chief Executive, BUPA (global healthcare)		x				x	x

Case Study 1
Richard O'Sullivan: Managing Director,
Millie's Cookies

Luck Indicators highlighted: all seven.

Richard O'Sullivan made his personal fortune through building and selling Millie's Cookies. Everyone knows Millie's Cookies: you can catch the aroma of those freshly baked cookies and taste the muffins at their outlets in just about every shopping centre, airport and train station in the UK.

How did he do it?

It was not a straightforward path. At the age of 17, he was catapulted into the workplace after his father had a stroke and could no longer work. By 19 he was married, and had bought his own restaurant in the centre of Manchester. At 23 he was bankrupt with a wife and two children to support. He had to sell his house, his car – everything. It took him several months to get back into employment.

The job he got was with Millie's Cookies. Less than two years later, in 1989, he bought the business; in 2003, he sold it for £25 million to Compass, a £12 billion company with over 400,000 employees. He is now managing the business during its integration process. No doubt he will looking for a new venture in the near future!

When describing his path to success, Richard O'Sullivan uses the words 'luck' and 'fortunate' a lot. Yet when you look more closely, it is easy to see that his kind of luck is not mere chance. In this Case Study we have analysed his story against all seven Luck Indicators. A summary of these appears on page 12.

What part did luck play in your success?

My first stroke of bad luck was when my father had a stroke

at 42 and never worked again. We had a really nice home and cars and swimming pool, and it all went. I was no longer 'heir to the throne', so I had to get out and do my own thing. In some ways it was good luck for me, because it forced me into the workplace at the age of 17.

Comment: He looked on bad luck as an opportunity (Percept-Ability – seeing the upside of every situation).

Can you give us an example of good luck?

A stroke of good luck was that when I was 19, I was working for a restaurant that went into receivership. I saw the opportunity and bought it from the receivers for £1. I ran this business for four or five years.

Comment: Another person in his position might well have seen this as a disaster and bemoaned the fact that they were unemployed. Again, great Percept-Ability.

What happened to that restaurant business?

I went bankrupt – I filed for personal bankruptcy at the age of 23. I lost everything. I sold my house, I sold my car – I sold everything. When someone comes in and takes stock of your furniture, you know you've hit rock bottom. And fortunately, at 23 I was able to bounce back from that.

Comment: An excellent example of Control-Ability. It's not the event itself that determines how lucky we are – it's our response to it. Richard bounced back.

At the moment of truth when you realised you were bankrupt what went through your mind? – How did you cope?

It took about three or four months for me to recognise that there was nowhere else to go. It's not as if I could go backwards. People can take away your house and your car, but they can't take away your education, your experience, your friends or your family. Being an entrepreneur is all about taking risks. If you're not willing to gamble, it's unlikely you're going to win, and buying a restaurant at 19 years of age was high risk. I finally recognised that this difficult experience was probably going to be a launch pad. The lessons I learned from it were fantastic, because I now surround myself with people who are excellent at what they do.

Comment: This response demonstrates how attitude to risk (Risk-Ability) can provide learning that leads to successful outcomes in the longer term.

Who do you blame for the failure of your restaurant business?

It was mine – absolutely 100% mine. There was no-one else involved. I was my own boss. I was a good operator, my customer base was growing, but the overheads were escalating and I wasn't long in the tooth enough to learn how to deal with debt, etc. The night I voluntarily shut the place down, I had a consortium of people who were prepared to put together the money to refloat it. But I wouldn't do that. It was a chapter in my life that was ready for closure.

Comment: High Control-Ability means accepting that where you are in life is a direct result of all your decisions to date. Richard took 100% responsibility for his actions and the subsequent results, and blamed no-one else. He also recognised when it was right to move on – an important part of Stick-Ability.

So how did you go from being flat broke and out of work to owning Millie's Cookies?

Luckily I was approached by an agency that told me about a new company called Millie's Cookies. They were looking for an operator and I seemed to fit the bill. I met up with them and I thought they had a huge amount to learn. Despite that, I joined them. I worked for them for 18 months and stuck it out regardless of how much I hated it.

I was lucky that the people who had invested their money in Millie's decided that the business was a non-starter. I saw this as an opportunity. They had half a dozen shops and I was fortunate enough to be able to put together a deal with a partner and buy them. It went from there to over 120 shops today.

Comment: Determination is part of Stick-Ability. Imagine if Richard had not been determined to bounce back: he might not have joined Millie's Cookies and he would not have got to where he is today. He also showed real Stick-Ability by staying in the job, which he hated, until an opportunity arose.

So what else makes you consider yourself lucky?

Well, I was particularly lucky regarding the sequence of events for getting some of the sites we bought. For example, the shop in Manchester was one of the first sites. It was hugely successful so we were able to build the business on it.

But really, the main lucky break was being in the right place at the right time – with the right attitude, I suppose. The fact that the original investors in the company lost interest in it and I was actually just there gagging for an opportunity was really fortunate. I just felt that buying the company was the right way to go. I'm quite scientific in how I make decisions, but most of the deciding factors are based on gut feeling – and a large part of the decision to buy Millie's was definitely gut feeling.

I was very fortunate. I don't know how much of it is luck and how much of it is just sheer determination, or a convergence of events that makes you who you are.

Comment: In this case, the convergence of events that Richard saw as 'lucky' was a result of his:

195

- ❖ *Stick-Ability – that is, his determination, and his ability to stick to the job in hand;*
- ❖ *high level of Percept-Ability, which meant he looked upon a potential disaster – being out of a job – as an opportunity. He made the impossible possible;*
- ❖ *Risk-Ability, which was also a key factor here – many people, having owned one failed business, would not have taken the huge risk of buying another one; and*
- ❖ *Sense-Ability – having his antennae out for opportunities and making a major decision based not only on facts but also on intuition.*

If I was to ask other people in your team what you have that's different or not the norm – what makes you lucky – what would it be?

One hundred per cent focus on my task above everything else in my life. Total, absolute, blinkered focus for me is mixed with determination. For me, it was the ability to get up in the morning every single day, day in, day out, and shovel whatever needed shovelling to do what we did and what we do.

The other thing is the human touch. I have 15 million customers and I still personally respond if there is a complaint. I work hard at the things that matter and, when you're dealing with your staff and managers, I recognise that it's all about the little things. It's the small things that upset them and the small things that also make them feel good – like remembering the name of their children. It's working with people and actually caring. I'd like to think that I do give a damn – certainly that's the way I like to be.

I have a surgery every Monday morning, when anyone in the company can pick up the phone, ring me direct and have

196

a chinwag with me. It doesn't have to be anything more than a chat. I actually love it when we're just having a chat.

I hope that I work to people's strengths. I've surrounded myself with people who have exceptional strengths in specific areas. By making the most of their skills, we just get the job done. I love working with people. For me, it's all about the human side of it.

I'd like to think that if I have a strength, it's the fact that I'm a good team leader. I'm not necessarily a great team player at all – I like to be leading the team. I suppose the joke is that my team will follow me anywhere, if only out of curiosity.

We also do a lot of healthchecks in the business, making sure that what *we* think is actually reality with the staff and managers. I'll have staff forums and sit around in a pair of jeans and T-shirt with staff, and find out what's going on. You learn an awful lot from that. You may not want to know the bad news but unfortunately it's a fact of life, and it's the only way we can learn and get a true gauge.

It's not possible to make a knee-jerk reaction to everything that happens: you have to have a measured view of things, so it's important to look for trends. The staff carries out 15 million customer transactions a year. Let's assume they know a little more about the customer and are little more important than I am. I make half a dozen decisions in a year of any worth – and that's it.

Comment: Stick-Ability is again obvious here in Richard's determination and focus. The other key Luck Indicator highlighted is Socia-Ability. Building a successful customer-facing business depends largely on the quality and attitude of the staff who meet the business. Being able to relate well to his team, listening to them and their views, suggestions and complaints, as well as making them valued and part of the business, have all played a key part in the growth and success of Millie's Cookies under Richard O'Sullivan.

Where does your motivation come from?

I think I've just been born and bred a retailer – that's all I've done all my life. My parents worked with supermarkets: even my mum had a flower shop and grocery store, so I've always worked in retailing. It's probably the only thing I can do! If you'd asked me when I was 18 or 20 what I'd be doing now, I just kind of figured that this is what I would be doing. I certainly knew that with my personality, I wasn't going to be a subordinate to many people, because I just rebel against that as a person. It's important to know yourself and where your strengths lie.

Comment: Note the high Person-Ability here – a true awareness of who he is and where his destiny lies.

Lucky tips

- ❖ Have total focus, determination and tenacity. Shovel what needs to be shovelled!
- ❖ Take risks, knowing that even if they go wrong, you will learn a great deal.
- ❖ Remember that you are totally responsible for yourself and your results. You cannot blame anyone or anything else.
- ❖ Do your homework – examine the facts and then do what feels right.
- ❖ Keep your eyes open – the best opportunities are often those that other view as 'bad luck' events.
- ❖ Recognise your strengths and surround yourself with excellent people who complement your skills. Make sure they know they are valued.

Case Study 2
Bhim Ruia: co-founder, the Ruia Group

Luck Indicators highlighted: Risk-Ability and Socia-Ability.

Bhim Ruia is co-founder of the Ruia Group, a successful family business that imports, supplies and distributes household textiles and hosiery to top UK retailers, wholesalers, hotels and hospitals. The company grew steadily from small beginnings in the 1950s and was so profitable that Bhim could afford to hand over the business to his sons and retire a wealthy man at the age of 50. He is now, as he puts it, a full-time lousy golfer!

How does a young man with few qualifications, who comes to England from his native India, build up a successful empire and heritage for his family? How much luck – if any – was involved? Bhim's story demonstrates many of the Luck Indicators. The two highlighted in this case study are Risk-Ability and Socia-Ability.

Bhim Ruia's approach to risk is an excellent example of how to manage the *level* of risk you take in order to ensure great returns over time. He had a clear risk strategy and stuck to it. There are two main aspects of Socia-Ability in Bhim's success story. One is his attitude to people and the other is the support of his family. Both were key factors in contributing to the success of the Ruia Group. In times of difficulty, in both personal and business matters, the family supported one another. As the business expanded, changes were done on a handshake and without the acrimony that is the hallmark of many businesses, whether family-run or otherwise. Look out for these two Luck Indicators in Bhim's story.

Bhim was a young man in India with an elder brother who had already moved to Manchester and set up an export textile business. Sending finished cloth to Africa was the basis of this business. An opportunity was spotted to dye and finish the raw cloth in England: this would not only attract a preferential duty charge, but would also produce a higher-quality product. The company began to do well and Bhim came to England to work in the business.

Not long after Bhim's arrival, something happened that many people would call bad luck. There was a sudden change in tax and tariff structures that meant that exporting to Africa was no longer possible. The company had to close or do something else. They decided to change their strategy and sell unfinished goods to local customers in the UK. Over the years this grew and developed, and was the basis of the successful company today

Adapting and responding to changing market conditions has been a feature of the company ever since. They have, over the years, expanded and developed into several different businesses that make a wide range of garments and other products.

Was it bad luck that the company almost folded when Bhim arrived? Bhim does not think so.

What is your view of luck and how it affected your business?
I think luck is a mythical thing. Luck doesn't exist. It's something we attribute to our modesty or arrogance, depending on where you sit. You have to work at what you want. A lot of success depends on being in the right place at the right time – and that means putting yourself about and looking after your customers.

Then, suppose you hit a bad time and it's not possible for you to make enough of a profit to be viable – then you begin to look for alternatives, for cheaper sources. What we did was to offer samples to potential customers, and got success with that. Slowly, slowly, profits and turnover increased. This is why I wouldn't say it was luck.

It's also to do with whether someone's face fits. You have to trust people to give them credit. I may not know someone, but somehow I'm confident that they won't let me down. That's what happened in our business.

You must have taken a large number of risks along the way ...

We did take many risks, but my attitude has always been to take a sensible approach to risk. In India, we have a saying: 'you spread your feet only according to the size of the sheet'. Thus, if the sheet is not long enough, your feet are exposed and you feel the draught – so you fold your feet under the sheet. What it means in terms of risk is that you only spend what you can afford or what you've earned.

It's also our philosophy that 'you can't dig a well to put out a fire' – by then, it will be too late. But if the well is already there, you can extinguish the fire. Similarly, if you want the facility to borrow money and you go to the bank at the last minute, you are unlikely to get what you want. It's essential to have a contingency plan.

My advice is therefore to set the credit line before you venture into a business deal. That gives you the limit of your exposure to risk. We always traded well within our limits. Some people believe that's silly because you can't optimise your money, but we believe that being within your limits doesn't bring pressure on you. You will never have sleepless nights.

So we lived within our means. We never took money out of the company for ourselves. We always made sure we had the facility to borrow from the bank but we did so as little as possible.

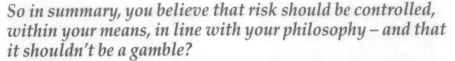

So in summary, you believe that risk should be controlled, within your means, in line with your philosophy – and that it shouldn't be a gamble?

Yes, I do. My grandfather lost all his money through speculation, so my father was against any kind of gambling. The important thing is to gamble or risk only the proportion of your assets that you can afford to lose without damaging the business.

What this meant for us was that we played within ourselves. We took a longer-term view than many other companies who, no matter how well they have done, only compare it with the same time last year. It makes me think of a joke that I heard recently: a tramp asked a passer-by for money, saying he had none. The passer-by, who happened to be an accountant, asked the tramp, 'how does this year compare to last year?' The tramp was left to reflect on the struggle he had had over the previous year, but without any financial help from the accountant.

We never did it that way. If we had a bad year, our philosophy was to simply acknowledge it and mentally set if off against many good years. The long-term strategic view really worked for us.

Lucky tips

- ❖ Spread your feet only according to the size of the sheet.
- ❖ Always dig the well before the fire starts.
- ❖ Look after your customers as well as you would your family.

Case Study 3
Tom Bloxham MBE: Group Chairman and co-
founder, Urban Splash

Luck Indicators highlighted: Risk-Ability and Percept-Ability. The difference between chance and luck is also a feature of this Case Study.

If you haven't heard of Urban Splash already, then it's likely that you will in the near future. In 1992, they didn't exist. Ten years later, their profits had grown by 74% a year from £1 million in 1999 to £5.2 million in 2002 – and are still growing. Being rated 24th in the *Sunday Times'* list of Britain's 100 Fastest Profit-Growth Firms 2004 is only one of a string of accolades awarded to the company.

Urban Splash redevelops inner city areas: for example, transforming derelict properties such as mills and warehouses into smart modern apartments. Every one of their property developments has won or been shortlisted for an award by the Royal Institute of British Architects.

Tom Bloxham has a list of personal awards too numerous to mention, including an MBE for services to architecture and urban regeneration in Manchester and Liverpool. As the Group Chairman and co-founder of Urban Splash, he began his entrepreneurial career by spending his first university grant cheque on records to set up a record business. When this was unsuccessful, he created a profitable poster business to supplement his grant. Along the way, he sold fire extinguishers door-to-door and ran a market stall before somehow finding himself in property development.

How much of this success story is due to luck? How does a graduate in politics and history end up being described as 'Britain's most famous property developer'? All the Luck Indicators can be spotted in Tom's story; the ones we have chosen to highlight here are Risk-Ability and Percept-Ability.

Tom Bloxham is all about being different, as the Urban Splash website testifies: 'Urban Splash is the developer behind the UK's most exciting urban regeneration projects. Our approach differs from the norm. We challenge convention. We design with imagination. Our buildings work for the people inside them – and the city beyond. Result: a catalogue of spectacular spaces where urban residents and workers thrive together.'

And with innovation, creativity and the desire to be different comes risk – in Tom's case, having the courage to take risks has certainly been true!

When we look at life with a 'can do' attitude, we spot opportunities that others miss. This is the cornerstone of the success of Urban Splash. Tom and his partner Jonathan Falkingham saw the potential in developing property that no-one else would touch with a bargepole. They turned this kind of property development into a trend that can now be seen all over the UK.

Over and above these two Luck Indicators, Tom's draws a distinction between luck and chance. He sees chance as what happens in life – things and events over which you have no direct control. Luck, on the other hand, is what you make of that chance happening.

Looking back, what motivated you to become successful?

I'm not sure. My father was in the Army and my mother a school secretary. They both went to college later in life. I was made aware at a very young age that the way to get on and avoid a lifetime of stacking supermarket shelves was to get an education – to go to university and get a decent job. However,

I've always enjoyed wheeling and dealing, buying and selling, and I guess that's got something to do with it.

One thing I can remember is running a market stall when I was a student. I was getting up at four or five o'clock in the morning, travelling halfway across the country. It involved a lot of quite heavy physical work and doing it all day made me exhausted. I remember making about £10 one day and I worked out that a person cleaning floors was making more money than I was. So I asked myself why I was doing it – and began to look for better and smarter ways to earn money.

In your view, what is the difference between people who are successful and those who are not?

Whatever the difference is, being successful doesn't happen by chance.

It's important to separate luck from chance. Most things in life are chance – where you live, who you are married to, the job you do – most of these are the result of chance events. The successful people grab the opportunities that chance throws up with both hands and use them. Less successful people dither and think, 'shall I do this, or shall I do that?', and don't take action. That's the difference.

You met your business partner Jonathan Falkingham quite by chance. Explain how you made the most of that opportunity.

When I was at university, my poster business was becoming very successful. I couldn't get my landlord to rent me space for it and that was when I got into property. Later on, I bumped into Jonathan. Between us we opened up a bar in a derelict property. We decided that if we could attract people to drink in such a place, how much better it would be if we could transform derelict properties with fantastic property design.

So was it luck that you were in the right place at the right time?

There were a lot of people in the same place at the same time as me and no-one else thought of doing what I did. What I've done is looked at what's around me and seen all sorts of lucky opportunities. For that reason, I tell everyone I'm the luckiest person in the world.

Someone once told me that luck is about creating a tidal wave. It's not what you buy and sell – it's about *when* you buy and sell. It's about *not* following the trend – it's about leading it. Following means just jumping on the bandwagon; but if you're ahead of the game, you can get yourself into a position where you are driving future trends. That's what I like.

You must have taken some huge risks when building up your business. What goes through your mind when things go badly wrong?

Well, for example, if a building contract is not going according to plan, first you think, 'Oh, shit, this is a pain – how am I going to deal with it?' But then the important thing is to get your head around it and say, 'Right, let's deal with it!' Usually you think, 'What's the worst possible thing that can happen?' Get that to the back of your mind, and think and say, 'That's that – we're going to accept it – now what can we actually do to improve the situation?' And as a bonus, it quite often happens that when you and your team are pulling together to deal with the crisis, it's actually quite good because it motivates people.

The important thing here, of course, is to surround yourself with brilliant people who will pull together as a team at all times.

What's the biggest risk you've ever taken?

There's been a whole succession right from the start. The

thing to do is to always consider the downside, measure that, go with your intuition and then control and manage the risk. The key thing is to make a decision. Sometimes it's possible to be too logical about decisions – to think too much about them – and do nothing.

What I always say is if you have to choose between decisions A, B and C, it doesn't matter which one you choose – just trust your instinct and go and do one. Some people can be *too* clever: they analyse everything but end up doing nothing. I like the Nike attitude – 'just do it'!

Lucky tips

- ❖ Look for the opportunity in every chance situation.
- ❖ Adopt a 'can do' mindset.
- ❖ Be bold – be ahead of the game. Be different and take risks that others might not. Just do it!
- ❖ Surround yourself with brilliant people.
- ❖ Remember that in every situation, there's something you can do to generate luck.

Case Study 4
Peter Donnelly: founder of the Eisenegger brand

Luck indicators highlighted: Control-Ability, Sense-Ability and Socia-Ability.

Peter Donnelly is a rough diamond. He is the son of a steel-worker, left school at 15 with no qualifications and worked on the road selling bedding and clothing from the back of a car for many years before founding the well known Eiseneg-ger brand of smart-casual and sports clothing. He retired at 50, a millionaire many times over. Eisenegger now has 60 branches throughout the UK and a turnover of over £50 million.

How did he do it? Was he just lucky? Did chances simply present themselves to him? Did the cards always fall right? No! Peter's story is one that demonstrates all the Luck Indicators, particularly Control-Ability, Sense-Ability and Socia-Ability. Check for these as you read his story.

Part of control is being totally independent, a feature of Peter's mindset throughout his career. Whatever he did was down to him alone. He relied totally on himself and his own judgement, and took the consequences whether good or bad.

Throughout his business life, Peter had an uncanny knack of being able to suss out the trends in fashion, to know when something was at the end of its life-cycle and to get in ahead of a new trend. At critical points in his life and career, he made decisions using only his intuition.

Peter is not an extrovert or a naturally sociable person, although the networking aspect of Peter's success is obvious. A fashion business such as Eisenegger is no good without a good supply line. Peter found the ideal solution – but not by chance. He networked.

So how does a steelworker's son with no qualifications become a wealthy and successful fashion designer?

When I was at school, I was a reasonably intelligent kid but a lot of my strengths lay in design and art, and that's what I wanted to do. I was particularly interested in clothing, so I decided to get into fashion. There were two obvious ways: one through the education route and the other by going into retailing. Instead of going to a further education college, I chose to leave home at 16 and go to work in retail menswear.

Where did your interest in fashion and design come from?

I don't know. My grandfather was in a business that was design-led but he died when I was five. It wasn't as if he was around till I was in my early 20s and got me set up in business or anything. I'm an only child. I left home – I was always independent, so I never had anyone to rely on. So if I was to put myself into circumstances then, I only had myself to get me out of them. I've always been independent for as long as I can remember.

What prompted you to take the non-academic route?

It was like a fork in the road – I just felt that the chances of being financially successful as well as being artistically fulfilled were better if I went it alone. I always believed that gut feel was a more overriding strength than business acumen. I didn't learn any business skills except through bitter experience!

So I got a job in haute couture – in the best operation outside London – and worked my way up. Then I came to a junction again. I considered going back to college as a mature student to do A Level art, but by that time I was 21, I'd bought my own house and I just felt I'd had too much freedom and I couldn't conform. I just couldn't do it.

What did you do next?

Well I sensed that the bespoke tailoring business was waning in this country. It was the start of off-the-peg, so I went to Germany, where brands were beginning to become the thing. I remember one of my friends, who worked for a major sporting company, played in a small Sunday morning football league in Germany. I went to watch them one day and was amazed to see the two teams who were kitted out in fantastic Olympic-quality strips provided by their employers.

I guess this was lucky, because it later gave me the idea of forming a company that specialised in branded sportswear.

You seem to be doing very well in your career at that point. When and how did you come to being on the road and selling things from the back of a car?

When my contract finished and I was waiting for a new posting in Bermuda, I came back to England. A friend of mine used to work on the road. He used to sell things from his car on the street – quilts, bedding and so on. It was the advent of the continental quilt. So we sold these quilts and made good money. By the time I was offered the job in Bermuda I had reached the conclusion that we needed to develop the selling business on a bigger and more organised basis. So I turned the Bermuda job down.

How did that lead to forming the Eisenegger brand?

Well, first of all, we went from selling quilts and bedding to selling the new trend – suedette jackets. When that trend died, we went into selling leather goods. Then when I sensed that the bubble was bursting and leather had run its course, that's when I sat down and started Eisenegger.

We needed a product. I remembered the Sunday morning football matches in Germany and spotted an opportunity in what was beginning to happen in sportswear at that time. When we started, Eisenegger was simply a tracksuit. Then we got some people out selling on the road and developed our product range; from there, we eventually managed to set up a unique supply line that meant I could sell more garments, and that lead to where we are today

Has luck – as you see it – played any part in your success?

Yes, it has. The biggest problem was the one I just mentioned – not being able to find a decent supply line for our goods. We had started a mail-order service and received awards for the products we came up with. We were struggling along until I stumbled into Manchester one day and happened to meet a friend of a friend who helped me solve the problem. Suddenly we were selling more jackets than anybody else.

So it's the old adage of the luck thing: the more you put yourself around, the more luck you get. It was a real lucky break, but in reality it wasn't actually luck – I was actively looking for a solution to the problem. It was the same when I was on the road working and selling out of a car – it was always a case of putting the time in and putting yourself about.

Is it just hard work? There are many people who work hard and are not successful ...

Hard work alone is not enough. I was always good at the branding thing. Whatever I was working hard at, I'd have a concept for it and I'd follow it all the way through from presentation to labelling. I was thorough, I suppose. I can't really see how it's luck – other than you're hitting the market with the right thing at the right time.

How do you know you're hitting the market with the right thing at the right time?

I don't know. It's a feel, isn't it – having a bit of a nose for what's in the air at the time.

So what is 'a nose for what's in the air'? If you were to advise someone how to develop it, what would you say?

I don't know. I didn't develop it myself – it was always there. My father was a steelworker, which was just about the most unrefined occupation and as big a contrast with what I did, so all I did was follow my passion and let that guide me.

Lucky tips

- ❖ Know what you are good at. Trust and follow your instincts.
- ❖ Be prepared to take the consequences of all the decisions you make.
- ❖ Be proactive in putting yourself about in such a way that you can find the right people to work with.

Case Study 5
Terry Flanagan: Chief Executive, Mason
Communications Group

Luck Indicators highlighted: Risk-Ability Socia-Ability and Person-Ability.

Terry Flanagan is one of those seemingly lucky people who seems to be successful at whatever he turns his hand to.

As well as co-founding and running a hugely innovative and successful telecommunications company, he has also achieved international status in the sporting world. Terry played rugby league for Britain, toured with the Lions in Australia in 1984 and has been an international rugby league coach.

Added to that, you may recognise him as one of the BBC TV rugby league commentary team. He loves to link the lessons and learning of sport to the business world

Mason Communications Group has grown from humble beginnings to win such accolades as being 36th in the *Sunday Times'* Best Company to Work For list and inclusion in the Guardian's Top 100 Innovative Companies.

As with all our other interviewees, it is possible to link Terry's success to all seven Luck Indicators. The three most obvious ones featured here are those of Risk-Ability, Socia-Ability and Person-Ability

Risk-Ability is not just about taking risks, it's about being innovative. It's about being confident enough to go for things and take action while others hang back till the window of opportunity closes. Hanging back was something Terry never did on the rugby pitch; if he had, he would not have achieved what he did. The same is also true of how Terry tackles his business.

Having high Risk-Ability doesn't mean jumping in without due thought, practice or preparation. It means balanc-

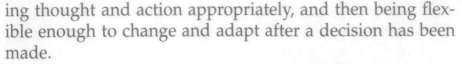

ing thought and action appropriately, and then being flexible enough to change and adapt after a decision has been made.

Business and social success depend greatly on our ability to interact successfully with others. This applies not just when you are at the bottom of the success ladder and aiming to make a name for yourself; it is an ongoing aspect of luck that needs to be attended to and developed. On a personal front, Terry has natural charisma – see Socia-Ability at work in his story.

Person-Ability can also be about having a clear sense of who we are and what we are doing. People who have high Person-Ability seem to have purpose – perhaps even a mission in life. Their confidence springs from knowing that who they are fits well with what they do – and what they like to do. This is certainly true in Terry's case.

Is luck a myth or a reality?

I think it's a reality, but at times I don't think it's as great as everyone makes out. There are many aspects to what people call luck: such as working 100%, being talented or having a good mix of personality, intellect, drive, energy, attitude and ability.

It's useful to remember that for all the lucky breaks you get, there are many unlucky breaks. My view is that it's not wise to dwell on the unlucky ones. I look to sports a lot for business leaning and analogies. I played at the top at sport and in my experience there is a high correlation between business and sport. I'm satisfied that giving everything your best shot is the number one factor in being 'lucky', but because a little bit of luck does come into it somewhere, when that happens you have to make the most of it.

Were you born with a silver spoon?

No. I was born of solid working class stock in a northern mill town with entrepreneurial parents. I put a lot of my formative early thinking down to watching my mum and dad have a go at various businesses, from greengrocer's shops to pubs. If something didn't work, they simply had another go. So watching and growing up in that environment, I learned that it was important to take risks. I definitely soaked up the entrepreneurial spirit – even if at the time I didn't realise it.

What was the biggest risk you ever took?

The biggest risk was starting the Mason Communications business. It was a case of investing one's house and career and having a go at it. I had no money and had to borrow it, but I felt confident enough to do it. I felt confident in creating my own luck and my own destiny, so the confidence was running high through the veins. I didn't let the demons get in the way. Looking back at it, I realise that it was potentially the highest risk of my career.

What do you mean by 'the demons'?

The demons are the voices of doubt in your mind that can sabotage your confidence. They give you all the reasons why you might fail at something. In my case, I was very determined to go for it. It's as if there's a demon on your right shoulder saying, 'And what happens if it doesn't work? What happens if you fail?' All those sorts of messages.

However, another voice – the upside demon, if you like – is saying, 'Don't be silly – you're smart enough, you have enough charisma, you work harder than most people. Stop being soft about it. You can do this if you want to.'

Now when this happens, you have a choice: you can listen to the doubting demon or the upside demon – that is, your true inner voice. Fortunately, I chose to listen to my inner voice – my gut feel. If I hadn't, I wouldn't be where I am today.

You mentioned the biggest risk you took. So are you suggesting that it's appropriate to take high risks all the time?

No. I think that the secret of taking risks is to look at the backdrop to where you are on your business evolution curve and your risk curve. Thus it's important to assess the type of risk that's in play depending on where you are. If you were a gambler and every year you bet your entire ranch on one contract, it would be unlikely to be sensible or successful. However, when you are young and flying by the seat of your pants, you might take that sort of risk. So timing and evolution are relevant.

So there are times at the start of a business, or any venture, when it might be entirely appropriate to stick your neck out and risk everything. But ten years down the line, if you were to go for something that might be a bit outside your reach, and there are other positive things going on in your business, then you might decide that this is too much of a risk and take a different, informed decision.

What drives you?

I was always driven by wanting to be successful and the best. I like to work on the ethic of giving everything your best shot. I always had that work ethic – which again, I guess I got from my parents, who encouraged me to study and gain qualifications because they had never had that chance.

I was lucky, therefore, in coming from a very supportive background where I learned the importance of making the most of all the opportunities that came my way. I worked 100% to get my O Levels, A Levels and university degree. There were many people around who were brainier than me, but they seemed to fall by the wayside dreaming about things whereas I rolled up my sleeves and got on with it.

What other factors have helped you achieve success?

Undoubtedly it's having good relationships with people. Being personable, having a great network, being able to build rapport quickly and understand the importance of first impressions in the first three to five minutes when you meet someone – all these are vital. In this business that's what we work hard at, and we endeavour to coach our staff in that. Because it's not just about the senior people in the team engaging with the Chief Executive of a client – it's about the members of my team consulting well with the members of the client's team. It's these sorts of personal skills we look and hunt for at Mason – and which we look to develop as well.

Lucky tips

- ❖ Take the learnings from sport: imagine life or business as a game.
- ❖ There's no shortcut to winning the game. Much of it is simply being committed, practising, working hard and *going* for it.
- ❖ Take different types of risk during the game depending on what the score is and where you are in the league!
- ❖ Make the most of opportunities and chances that occur during the game. Many poor scores and lost games are due to not maximising the chances presented to the team.
- ❖ Consider yourself as part of a team: not just your own side on the pitch, but also your supporters and your sponsors. If you look after them, they will look after you.

Case Study 6
Lal Kumar: Chairman, Rajan Imports

Luck Indicators highlighted: Risk-Ability and Socia-Ability.

The son of a wealthy doctor and businessman, Lal Kumar's world was shattered when his father's wealth vanished at a stroke and the family were left with nothing. The year was 1947, the historic time when India was divided. The family fled from the riots to live in Delhi. His father's wealth was tied up in the property left behind and the family became penniless.

At that time, Lal was only 15 years old and at school. Despite the family poverty, he continued at school, went on to college and finally graduated. At 20, still with no money, he set sail for England by the cheapest possible means of transport – a boat that took 20 days to complete the journey. In England, he set up a market stall selling stockings. Two years later, he bought his first car; two years after that, he bought and paid for – *in full* – his first house. He is now a millionaire and has a flourishing international export business, with branches in London, Manchester, Düsseldorf, Hong Kong and New York

Lal puts some of his success down to luck, but when it's analysed, it is clear that his luck is not due to mere chance. The Luck Indicators most noticeable in Lal's success story are Risk-Ability and Socia-Ability.

Many people assume that risk is all about financial gambles, but sometimes the greatest risks are more to do with flying in the face of traditional wisdom and having the courage to approach a situation from your own point of view.

The business empire built by Lal Kumar over the years was largely successful due to his attitude to people in the widest sense. Socia-Ability in this broad sense includes the motivation to build up a secure future for your family, using the network or community, becoming known by your customers and trust-

218

ing people – customers and suppliers alike. In the beginning, Lal was only able to start and then grow his business because he trusted others and they trusted him. It's true that what goes around, comes around!

How were you able to start up a business when you arrived in England with almost nothing?

I stayed with a relative for a short spell and started earning money by selling stockings on a market stall.

I could do this because my relative introduced me to a few people. It wasn't a question of being supported by him; nobody supported anybody as such at that time because nobody could. The main aim was to earn enough money to pay your rent and your food bill.

There were a number of Asians who were already selling stockings at that time, so it was easy to get goods on credit from other wholesalers who were also Asians. Most people knew everybody, so they could trust you for small amounts of credit. Once you established yourself, they would give you more. I guess it was a kind of network.

For my part, after getting started I paid for everything by cash. I've always believed in having no credit because then you're not wasting money on high interest. Another thing: if you have no money, you can't afford to buy heavy goods such as knitwear or anoraks and tie your capital up. With stockings, you could put them in a suitcase and jump on the bus, which was easy. Later on, as the business built up, I was then able to sell a wider range of goods.

Did you ever think at that time where your business would lead?

No! At that time I had no goals. I never thought in my wildest dreams that I'd become a millionaire. In fact, I had no dreams. How can you have goals and dreams when you're working in the markets – in the cold, wet and snow, trying to sell things to make just enough money to make ends meet?

So what changed?

Despite having no dreams at the start, I began to realise that I wanted to do better than some of the people around me, who were content with their small businesses. I suppose I always had a bit of a business mind. Also, about that time I got married.

My wife went with me to the markets. I remember it was a very, very cold day and despite wearing fur boots and a few sweaters, my hands were shivering. I was putting sheets on the market stall and my wife said, 'There must be a business where you don't have to stand in the markets.' I said, 'Yes, I'll have to find something.'

That's when I opened my first cash and carry warehouse. I set it up in a location that was well away from where all the Asians used to trade. I was laughed at, but I reckoned that because I was less well off than the other traders, I would be able to carry less stock and therefore be unable to compete with them. People used to laugh, but I decided I would go for a different part of the market – for non-Asian customers. I did well there.

Where did luck fit in – if at all?

Luck did come into at a little bit … I was lucky to find a market – a very good market – where I was known. People used to ask for me by name and I built up a very solid customer base.

I was also very lucky to be from a nice family and to be able to show that I could be successful in business when it came to marrying the woman I wanted. My father was a very learned person. He would tell me you have to be honest with people, and I have passed that on to my children. So I am very lucky with my wife and family.

Finally, perhaps I am lucky too with the people I have dealt with along the way. There are all sorts in the world – but you have to trust people. If you don't trust them, you can't survive in business – especially in our business, where we give credit to everybody.

My motto since I started my wholesale business is to always give people the benefit of the doubt and build relationships with people, so that over time you can always get the amount you lend back. Some of my friends used to tell me I was mad to give everyone credit. My thinking was different – I knew people would come back to me and pay off as much of their credit as possible in order to be able to buy more goods. This paid off for all of us.

What is it that motivates you?

The day your children come into the business, all your dreams are fulfilled. This is what I have worked for all my life – thinking about what my children will have when they grow up. Now they run the business and are very good at it.

Lucky tips

- ❖ Remember that anything is possible if you set your mind to it.
- ❖ Have a strong motivation for succeeding.
- ❖ Listen to others but if in doubt, stand up for what *you* believe to be the best or right course of action.
- ❖ Look after, trust and appreciate the people around you – your customers, creditors, networks and, most of all, your family. As someone once said, 'The only way to know if a man is trustworthy is to trust him.'

Case Study 7
Andy Gilbert: Group Managing Director, Go MAD
Research & Consulting Group

Luck Indicators highlighted: Control-Ability, Sense-Ability Socia-Ability and Person-Ability.

Andy Gilbert is Group Managing Director of the Go MAD Research & Consulting Group and developer of the internationally recognised Go MAD® thinking system, which describes the common factors to success.

He set up his business in 1997. In the first year of trading, he was able to afford to give 50% of his profits away to charity. The business flourished. By 1999, he had formed an educational charity Go Make A Difference (Go MAD), offering free training to young people to learn the success principles embodied in his thinking system. Andy has not lost out from his charitable interests – far from it. The business is hugely successful and has gone from strength to strength, based on the application of the success principles that underpin it.

Andy is not one of those people who says one thing and acts differently. He lives the way he thinks. He knows his system works – the research has proved it and so has he. Many of the success factors identified by Andy correlate strongly with the Luck Indicators in this book. Andy's story in full covers all seven of the Luck Indicators; in this Case Study we are focusing on four, although you are sure to spot more as you read. These are Control-Ability, Sense-Ability, Socia-Ability and Person-Ability.

In essence, Control-Ability is about believing that it is possible to create your own destiny and your own success. Andy has developed this to a fine art. No matter how difficult the situation he is faced with, he finds a way to flex his behaviour in order to get the most from it.

222

A common misconception is that having high Socia-Ability means being an extrovert. This is not necessarily the case – as Andy demonstrates. One of the aspects of Socia-Ability highlighted in Andy's story is its charitable focus – reaching out into the wider community. Many people would view this as a distraction from the commercial aims of a business, but Andy would claim it has simply added to his success. 'Giving something back' is one of his values and that's what makes it work.

How much has luck been a factor in your success?

Not at all. For example, at the time when I was setting the business up, I had a very high self-belief – like a nine out of ten that I was going to negotiate a deal that would give me the financial security I needed for at least the first six months. So there was no luck in that. It was down to me and the skill of my selling. Then after that, it was still up to me to develop the business and make it successful.

To take another example, people said we were lucky to have happened to spot a wonderful property to invest in – but actually, it wasn't luck, because when you've got a goal and you're focused on it, you just become more aware of the opportunities that lead you towards your goal. The fact is that yes, we had been looking for a property, and yes, the right one did seem to come along.

Do you think there are some people who are naturally more able to set and achieve goals than others – people who seem to set off on a fast track to success?

Well this goes back to nurture versus nature. I'm a big fan of 'nurture', because I haven't come across a baby so far that can define goals for itself – all of those types of skills are nurtured. Now yes, we might be born into certain environments – if there is luck, then that's where it is.

So I would put luck down to being the sperm that enters the egg and being dealt the set of cards given to you by your parents at that particular time and place. I think that I was lucky to be born in the UK as opposed to other places in the world. I was lucky in that I didn't choose or influence my parents. Apart from being a determined sperm, that was as far as it went!

What else has contributed to your success?

Relating to people is key. In my childhood, I didn't find this easy. I wasn't a natural extrovert, but I realised the importance of communication skills and good listening skills. These are areas an individual can choose to develop.

I know some very good networkers that are highly social. In actual fact they are naturally introverted, but they realise the benefits of networking – even if it's well outside their comfort zone. And the funny thing is, the more often you go outside that comfort zone and get that experience, the more comfortable it becomes. So for me, it all comes down to taking personal responsibility to develop myself.

One of the things I now do when I am in a social or professional environment is to look for two interesting people and one useful thing that I can apply. I love people, so I'm always thinking – who is the interesting person here? Tracking that back, I'm asking myself good quality questions. And what I find is that if you look for interesting people, you'll find them!

You seem to place a high value on thinking. Where does gut feel fit in?

There's no substitute for quality thinking. However, gut feel has a real part to play. My view is that gut feel is based on all your experiences in life that are collected at an unconscious level. That's why you can trust that your subconscious is telling you something.

Let me give you an example. In our lives, we have probably met tens of thousand of people. We have seen tens of thousands more on TV. So we know that we have a huge number of reference points for nice people, nasty people, honest and dishonest people, and so on. The more reference points, the better the picture it is possible to build up. All these experiences have been absorbed so that when we meet a person for the first time, we are subconsciously measuring them against all past reference points. But we don't go through a checklist; we just trust the feeling that gives us the information. For me, it's something that has been built up through experience.

Are there any instances where you came up against real obstacles and you had to work hard to overcome them – things that others described as bad luck?

Loads of them – including missed opportunities that have cost me millions. For example, I had a massive contract that was poised to come to fruition the week following the 9/11 disaster. We'd been working on this for a year. The event was cancelled and never rearranged.

How did you cope with that mentally in terms of your response?

I coped well, because of knowing the stuff that I know about making a difference. You know you have to control the way you think. What you do is say to yourself, 'I have got choices in what I do. I can either point the finger of blame and say "Woe is me", or I can say "It's a given".' I use that phrase a lot. The good thing about history is that it's all in the past. That's why it's a given and you can't change it. But you *can* change your response to it. So when this event happened, I chose to

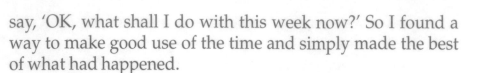

say, 'OK, what shall I do with this week now?' So I found a way to make good use of the time and simply made the best of what had happened.

Many people will read this and may not believe that such a cool response is possible. Was it honestly as simple as that? What was your initial response before your controlled response kicked in?

You need to remember that I am an extreme example. It takes me only one or two seconds to get over any initial shock. I've simply trained myself to say, 'it's a given' – because that is the most helpful thing I can say to myself.

In your first year you made a profit and you gave 50% of it away – why did you do that?

That's to do with my values. Building a business is not just about selling. I wanted to give something back to young people who might never have the chance to go on a management or leadership development programme, or work for a large organisation. That's why I did it: it's to do with thinking that it would have been great if I had learned some of that good stuff when I was younger.

I guess it comes from my upbringing, my father being a minister and my mother a special needs school teacher. So combining the two, you have solid values combined with the importance of education. As a result, I've always done a lot of voluntary work. When you are fortunate, I always feel that giving something back is the right thing to do. Living in line with your values is very important to me. It frees me up to perform well in all areas of my life.

Lucky tips

- ❖ Have clear goals and know why you want them. If you focus on them, the opportunities will come your way.
- ❖ Believe in yourself. Success is not out there waiting: it's up to you to take action and go for what you want.
- ❖ Take personal responsibility for developing yourself and pushing the boundaries of your comfort zones.
- ❖ Find a way to choose a helpful response to events when they go against you.
- ❖ Be true to your values.
- ❖ Give to others without expecting any reward.

Case Study 8
Val Gooding CBE: Chief Executive, BUPA

Luck Indicators highlighted: Stick-Ability, Percept-Ability and Person-Ability.

Val Gooding is one of the most senior women in Britain. She has a long list of impressive credentials. As well as being Chief Executive of BUPA, the UK's leading independent healthcare company, she is also a non-executive director of both BAA PLC and Compass Group PLC, and she sits on the Council of Warwick University and the Advisory Board of the Warwick Business School. She is a Trustee of the British Museum and President of the International Federation of Health Plans.

Val was awarded the CBE for services to business in the 2002 New Year's Honours list and is regularly cited as one of the UK's most powerful women.

How did she achieve this level of success? Was it luck? Her story is an inspiration to men and women alike. It proves that anyone can get the success they aim for if they have complete determination and the relevant ability and attitude.

The key Luck Indicators to look out for in Val's story are Stick-Ability and Percept-Ability.

Val made her mark in a man's world. By persevering through the bad times as well as the good, Val reached senior levels in the airline industry, where women were rare. Val's rise to the top was a result of her ability to make the most of any situation she was in and any opportunity that presented itself. It began at a time when women simply did not get senior management jobs in business. In fact, most women did not *believe* it was possible. Val was different. Her belief in herself meant that she did not look at her prospects in that light.

Breaking through the glass ceiling to get a position in senior management was surely one of her biggest achievements.

Val's career progressed slowly but steadily as she rose through the ranks in the airline industry – she was not on some privileged fast-track scheme. However, her inner conviction that she was always capable of doing more and better finally paid dividends. She was a good judge of her own capabilities and applied that same judgement to all the Luck Indicators. Excellent self-awareness has been a key factor in Val's success, along with ability, hard work and determination.

Where – if anywhere – does luck feature in your success?

There is some good fortune involved in having a stable family background and a brain. Other than that, it's been all hard work.

There is a tendency, in women especially, to say, 'Oh, I've just been lucky – I've just been in the right place at the right time.' The truth is that in my case, you can't say luck plays no part, but on the other hand most of it has been hard work.

Also, while there have been times when I've been in the right place at the right time, quite often I've been in the wrong place at the wrong time and things have gone backwards for me.

What did you do when things went wrong for you or you were in the wrong place at the wrong time?

There have been many times in my career when – because of competitive processes, reorganisations or upheavals, management changes, and so on – I ended up with a job that was not the job I would have ideally chosen.

In those circumstances I was aware that I had quite clear choices to make. I could either say, 'I haven't got the job I would ideally like, therefore I'm not accepting it and I'm going to leave and seek employment somewhere else.' Or I could say, 'Well actually, this could be interesting. I think I'm going to have a go at it and see how it turns out.' I always took the latter option. And the odd thing is that most of the options that I thought wouldn't be so interesting turned out to be really interesting – much more interesting than what I might have chosen.

So when I've had setbacks like this, I've tried to be optimistic and think, 'OK, this is still a very good job and it could be very interesting, so why don't I have a crack at it and see if it turns out to be exciting and worthwhile?' – and it has been!

Where does your inner drive come from?

I'm not sure where it comes from. Maybe it's genetic – it's in your DNA. It's not something you entirely have control over.

For me, it's just that I always felt I could do something bigger. For example, every so often I would come across someone doing a much more senior job and I would think, ' I could do that job just as well – or maybe even better!' So I think that tends to inspire you to think, 'If I'm persistent here, perhaps I could get the opportunity to do one of these jobs.'

Also, I used to get a feeling inside myself if I'd reached a stage in a job when I was treading water and not being stretched or challenged, when I would think to myself that I must be able to do something bigger than this.

Looking back, how do you see your career?

I often think of my career in terms of the tortoise and the hare. I was the tortoise: my progress was incredibly slow and I spend a long time plodding along in very mundane jobs that I did to the best of my ability. But I hung in there and never accepted that that was going to be my level of achievement. I always thought, 'I can do more than this.'

The other analogy that seems to fit my career is the Greek myth about Sisyphus, who pushed a boulder all the way up a hill; just when he got to the top of the hill, it rolled down again. In a way, that is my metaphor for what you need to do if you're working in any kind of business situation. Things are not always easy and often, the first time you try them, they don't work.

It's the same with people's careers. The first time they try to make a breakthrough or a change, or get a promotion, or get headhunted by another company, it may not work – or the second time or the third. Eventually – unlike Sisyphus – you *can* get to the top and see the boulder running down the other side.

Lucky tips

- ❖ Never give up. Experience shows that patience and perseverance are often rewarded.
- ❖ Always aim to see a value and a meaning in what you are doing, even at times when the job – or whatever you are doing – is boring or not stretching you.
- ❖ Find a way to look at an unsatisfactory situation till you can see why it's relevant and important, and why it needs to be done. Then bring your own special contribution to it.
- ❖ What looks like bad luck is often good luck in disguise. As the Dalai Lama said, 'Remember that not getting what you want is sometimes a wonderful stroke of luck.'

Luck in Your Business

Teams who share the qualities of lucky people will be high-achieving and aspirational, and will be the ones who make the business model work.

If you would like to know more about how to attract these people into your organisation and how to make sure you get the best out of them – ensuring that they achieve their full potential using the powerful tools we have explored in this book – then get in touch with us via our website, **www. switchtosuccess.co.uk**.

Alternatively, you can contact us by e-mail on **heather@ switchtosuccess.co.uk** or **anne@switchtosuccess.co.uk**.

Index

INDEX

Schulz, Will 180
self-awareness 49, 171–80,
182–8
self-fulfilling prophecy (SFP)
144–5, 158–61
Sense-Ability 13
Brilliant Ideas 98–108
communication channels 98
creating 96–8
definition 91
emotional honesty 105
gut feel/intuition 91–2, 94–5
having/not having 96–8, 99
heightened awareness 92–5
listen to your body 102–3
take a chance 104
time of day test 100
time out 101
what it means 91–6
shredder technique 39
Situation-Response-Consequence
(S+R=C) 24–5, 177
six degress of separation 114
'Sleeping Beauty' mindset 18–19
SMART 57
snapshot teqhnique 35–6
Socia-Ability 13
Brilliant Ideas 126–37
creating 120 22
definition 113
having/not having 120–22,
123
networking 114–20
what it means 113–20
sport 51
Stick-Ability 12
awareness 46–7
Brilliant Ideas 55–62

choice 47
definition 43
determination/stubborness
44–6
free flowing/drifting 50
having/not having 52–4
if only's 52
relationships 50–51
sport/business 51
tenacity/perseverance 43–4,
49–50
testing 47–50
what it means 43–51
Stone, Glenda 137–40
stress 98, 100, 106
stretching principle 19
success
creating
Control-Ability 27–8
Percept-Ability 151–3
Person-Ability 178–80
Risk-Ability 73–6
Sense-Ability 96–105
Socia-Ability 120–22
Stick-Ability 52–3
definition 2
mindset 20–21
in practice 2–3
reasons/excuses 21–2
Sullivan, Richard 191
luck indicators 192
luck in practice 193–8
lucky tips 198

Thompson, Mark 92
Toon, David 71–3
Trickett, Jon 168–9
Tucker, Colin 14–16

239

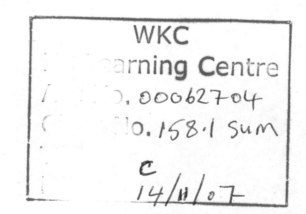